# OLD
# IRONSIDES

G·K
Hall
&C°.

*Also by Edwin P. Hoyt*
*in Large Print:*

Against Cold Steel
Hellfire in Tripoli
Decatur's Revenge

This Large Print Book carries the
Seal of Approval of N.A.V.H.

# OLD IRONSIDES

## EDWIN P. HOYT

G.K. Hall & Co. • Thorndike, Maine

Published in 2000 by arrangement with Wieser & Wieser, Inc.

G.K. Hall Large Print Paperback Series.

The text of this Large Print edition is unabridged.
Other aspects of the book may vary from the original edition.

Set in 16 pt. Plantin by Minnie B. Raven.

Printed in the United States on permanent paper.

**Library of Congress Cataloging-in-Publication Data**

Hoyt, Edwin Palmer.
  Old Ironsides / by Edwin P. Hoyt.
    p.  cm.
  Originally published: New York : Pinnacle Books, 1976.
  Includes bibliographical references.
   ISBN 0-7838-9151-2 (lg. print : sc : alk. paper)
   1. Constitution (Frigate)  2. United States — History, Naval —
To 1900.  3. Large type books.  I. Title.
VA65.C7 H64  2000
  359.3'22'0973—dc21                                    00-044836

# OLD IRONSIDES

Ay, tear her tattered ensign down!
   Long has it waved on high,
And many an eye has danced to see
   That banner in the sky;
Beneath it rung the battle shout,
   And burst the cannon's roar; —
The meteor of the ocean air
   Shall sweep the clouds no more!

Her deck, once red with heroes' blood,
   Where knelt the vanquished foe,
When winds were hurrying o'er the flood,
   And waves were white below,
No more shall feel the victor's tread
   Or know the conquered knee; —
The harpies of the shore shall pluck
   The eagle of the sea!

O better that her shattered hulk
   Should sink beneath the wave;
Her thunders shook the mighty deep,
   And there should be her grave;
Nail to the mast her holy flag,
   Set every threadbare sail,
And give her to the god of storms,
   The lightning and the gale!

Oliver Wendell Holmes 1830

# TABLE OF CONTENTS

# INTRODUCTION

No part of a nation's history is as interesting or as crucial as its beginning for this is the time a nation sets its course, determines its principles and establishes the foundations for its future.

In the 1790s the fledgling United States had little economic power, no military strength and slight influence on events in the world. At the close of the Revolution she was not taken seriously by any other nation and she existed by the sufferance of European nations that had more important matters to consider than the weak United States.

The story of *Constitution* is the fascinating story of how dedicated men helped create respect and prestige for this new nation. Edwin Hoyt has captured the spirit of the times. He understands that a man-of-war takes on the characteristics of the men who serve in her. Her reputation becomes the conglomerate repute of her actions; the many actions of *Constitution* brought fame and glory to her — and respect and esteem to the country she served so long and so well. To this day she has become a symbol of the courage, spirit, and hard-won success of the Americans who formed a great country — and her story is their story — the story of our predecessors.

It all began when Americans came to realize

that both participants in the Anglo-French war were using our territory and even our people to fight their wars, with complete disregard to treaties, to our wishes, our neutrality or our sovereignty. There wasn't anything we could do about it except protest — and pass neutrality acts which we could not enforce. We had no power and France and Britain as well as the Barbary States continued to seize our merchant ships on the high seas and treat our protests with disdain.

At long last a Navy was authorized. Fortunately, the ingenious Joshua Humphreys was chosen to design four frigates. He gave them speed and heavy guns — and he built *Constitution*. He was the first man to put his mark on his ship for he built a strong sturdy frigate with good solid workmanship, superior to frigates of other nations.

Good ships are important, but it is men who win battles. The men who manned *Constitution* were as sturdy as their ship. With weeks and weeks of grilling work at sea they forged a battle-ready ship able to defeat a skillful, experienced enemy. Then, as crews changed, often they did it all over again to retain competent professionalism.

The captains instilled into those officers and men the other characteristics required by a man-of-warsman — discipline, courage, audacity, and enthusiasm. As *Constitution* won her battles, sometimes against great odds, the French and the Barbary pirates and finally the British learned from bitter experience that the United States was not a feeble, ineffectual little nation they could tyrannize. Over the years *Constitution* helped the United States gain recognition of her sovereign rights, and other nations accorded to ship and nation the honor and esteem they had earned. Many officers and men, trained in *Constitution*, went to other ships, and continued creating the great traditions of our early Navy.

Mr. Hoyt has recorded vividly and truly the inspiring history of a great ship — and great men.

Admiral Arleigh Burke, USN Ret.
February, 1976

# CHAPTER ONE

## THE FIGHTING SHIP

In the early winter months of 1794 the Philadelphia naval architect Joshua Humphreys was sorely troubled, like many another American, because his country lay defenseless on the seas. The little United States of America had no navy, and so her merchant ships were prey to every pirate on every sea across the world.

The center of the trouble was the Levant, the area in the Mediterranean that was ruled by the Turkish sultan, though only half so. The vassal kings of Algiers, Tripoli and a half-dozen other Barbary ports were little powers unto themselves. They sent their pirate vessels out across the Mediterranean. And naturally those pirates concentrated on attacking the ships of nations that had no effective defenses. The Barbary pirates soon learned to respect the Union Jack — the Royal Navy taught them that in a hurry. And the French were growing aggressive and punitive in their actions as well.

But the United States in the early 1790s had not a single ship with which to defend itself abroad. No sooner had the war of independence come to an end than the thirteen original colonies had abandoned the idea of common defense in the lack of apparent need. All the naval vessels built during the war were paid off and sold off. And since that time, hundreds of Americans had been caught and imprisoned by the Barbary pirates. The American government had paid out hundreds of thousands of dollars in ransom to get those men freed.

For four years thoughtful men had tried to secure action from a divided Congress. President George Washington had presented the facts on the Algerian pirates and their plunders in 1790. Two years later the Americans were still paying tribute, and the arrogant Dey of Algiers actually refused to receive an American representative. By that time, the more powerful nations of the world had all made treaties with Algiers.

"If I were to make peace with everybody," said the Dey plaintively, "what should I do with my corsairs?"

What should he do, indeed! His idea was to scour the Mediterranean and even go outside to the Canaries and along the European coast to find American ships to plunder and American captives to ransom.

By 1793 the merchants of American ports were worried lest the corsairs soon begin lying off the American coast to await victims.

In October came the word that eight Algerian pirate ships had captured eleven American vessels and one hundred six American sailors.

"Another corsair on the Atlantic; God preserve us!" wrote the American consul from Lisbon.

The word brought panic to Philadelphia and Boston, New York and Baltimore, the growing trade ports whose ships were fanning out across the world. The panic brought renewed pressure on the American government, and caused men like Joshua Humphreys many anxious hours. Humphreys was a Quaker; nonetheless his pen began toying with a design for a warship. The bad news speeded his efforts, and it was not long before he evolved a design. And what a warship! It was to be superior in fighting qualities and speed to anything afloat that was anywhere near its size. It could deal with the Xebecs of the corsairs offhandedly; it could challenge and conquer any warship on the seas save the huge ships of the line of the European sea powers, and it should run away from one of those like a child escaping a lame grandmother.

While Joshua Humphreys fretted in the taverns of Philadelphia, along with the other men who earned their livelihood from pursuits connected with the sea, masters and traders and families of men imprisoned were importuning Congress for action. It came on March 27, 1794, in a bill authorizing the construction of four big frigates and two smaller ones. Soon Humphreys' plans were shown to be superior to those of other architects, and they were accepted. The decision was made by Henry Knox, the Secretary of War — there was no Navy Department then.

Joshua Humphreys set out to build one ship himself, and to supervise the construction of the others in a loose sort of way.

One of them, to be called *The Constitution*, was assigned to Boston, and Hartt's Naval Yard in Boston harbor was given the basic contract for a hull that was to be 204 feet long over all, 43.6 feet breadth of beam, and drawing 23 feet of water. To see what Humphreys had done, consider this: the standard British frigates were 180.3 feet long, 38.8 feet in the beam, and shallower.

Humphreys knew precisely what he was doing. He was building ships that could outgun the British and French frigates without any question. The wonder was that no one had thought of doing this earlier; it took a young nation without the old strictures to accomplish something so simple.

Humphreys was thinking ahead, not of the Barbary corsairs, which were an immediate but not vital problem, but of the French and British fighting navies that were sure to cause Americans trouble as their struggle for dominance in Europe overlapped into the waters of the Americas. France and Britain both laid claim to parts of Canada, and both nations had imperial colonies in the Caribbean. So any American who thought about such matters must know that the quarrels were bound to wash over America.

The number and variety of sailing ships in the late eighteenth century was tremendous, but naval usage cut the fighting ships down to three basic types: sloops, frigates, and ships of the line.

A sloop was any gunned ship whose guns were carried on its upper deck. It was as simple as that; it made no difference how many masts or sails the vessel had.

A frigate carried its guns on the main, or gun, deck. Some additional guns were carried above on the forecastle and quarterdeck. Guns were very heavy, and so while twenty-eight or thirty guns would be mounted on this lower deck, it would be suicidal to overbalance the ship with so much weight above. Consequently on the upper deck, a frigate usually carried only six or eight guns fore and aft, perhaps to fight in chases or to menace shore installations.

A ship of the line might have three or four decks of guns, might carry as many as a hundred — even more — and was a huge, awkward floating fortress that was hard to manage in heavy seas.

So when the ingenious Joshua Humphreys considered the American problem with no navy at all, and the need to defend against the certainty of British and French involvements in the future, he designed a vessel that was bigger than the second class of European ships. What was wanted, he wrote a friend, was a ship that in blowing weather would be an overmatch for the enemy's double-deckers, or frigates, and in light winds could sail faster and escape a whole squadron of them. In blowing weather, the ship he had in mind would outmatch even a ship of the line, and in calm weather she could outsail them.

He was talking about *The Constitution* and her sister ships, as he envisaged them.

Now to build them was something else again, and it would call for the highest skills of the artisans of the young American republic. Colonel George Claghorn was appointed to be naval constructor, and when he saw what he had to do, he whistled, for he was one of the first to recognize what a major revision Humphreys was bringing to the world of fighting ships. Later the British were to complain that the American frigates were not frigates at all, but "razeed seventy-fours." A seventy-four was a ship of the line, and to razee meant to take off the top deck. It was true, Humphreys had the timbers and the masts and spars made of the same strength as the bigger ships — and Colonel Claghorn had to do the job.

One of the first tasks was to secure the woods. She should be built of red cedar and live oak and fine straight pine. Colonel Claghorn and his assistants looked about for someone who could be trusted to find these woods. John T. Morgan, a master shipwright of Boston, was chosen. He had supervised the hull building of dozens of sturdy fast vessels, and he knew his timber as did few others in the Bay State. Morgan was soon dispatched to Savannah and Charlestown, for this section of the southern coast had the finest shipbuilding woods in the Americas known to the young Republic.

Morgan went with an importunation from the

Secretary of War. He was to find everything in his own country. *Constitution*, like all other frigates, was to be built entirely of native materials, even the iron for the cannon and the hemp for the rope was, ideally, to come from American sources. It was a proud dream.

So Morgan took local people and their slaves into the forests and found his woods. Off the mouth of the Altamaha river on the island of St. Simon was a fine stand of native oak, tall and stout and hard of line. Here the first tree was felled, and the stump was marked out by the celebrants, from that time on to be known as Constitution Oak. The log and dozens like it were rafted and loaded aboard ship to join scores of other logs of cedar and pine, and shipped up to Boston, and the work commenced, as General Henry Jackson, the naval agent in Boston, paid out the sums for the logging and the shipping.

The keel was laid down at Hartt's yard, and the other work contracted out to local builders. Edmund Thayer won the bid for the gun carriages, stout wooden supports to hold the long guns that would nose through the ports of the frigate's gun deck. A nearby mastyard built the three great masts, the long bowsprit, and the spars, and all the spares with which she would be equipped to begin her fighting career.

The anchors were built at Hanover (Massachusetts), near an iron mine and a foundry, but most of the work was carried out around Boston itself, with Paul Revere, the metalsmith, supplying the copper sheathing that would keep the worms out of the hull, and the copper bolts and spikes that were needed in points of stress where there must be no chance of the failure of iron through oxidation.

The sails were made in a loft that would later be called the Granary Building, at the corner of Park and Tremont streets. The figurehead and the other ornamentation of the ship were made by the talented Skillings Brothers. But the hemps and the guns — these were another matter. Young America was not so skilled in the arts of war as all that — the first guns bore the imperial stamp *GR*, which meant they came from *Georgius Rex*'s English foundries.

The guns would be changed many a time, and American gunsmiths and cannonmakers later would be able to take all the pride they wanted over the years in their contributions to *Constitution*.

By the end of the first year all the timber was in hand, and the carpenters and smiths were shaping and bending, bolting and fastening. In October the workmen were beginning to talk about the day when the vessel would be ready for launching.

Then came a blow.

The bill in Congress permitting the construction of the warships had been fought all the way by those who saw no reason to spend the nation's money on warships or defense of any kind. These opponents of military preparedness believed that through negotiation and strict neutrality the United States had no reason to worry about war. True, the depradations of the Barbary pirates had swayed enough votes in 1794 to cause the building of these ships, but those who hated the idea of preparation for war still despised that idea, and were waiting for a chance to reverse the position.

The opportunity came in the fall of 1795. For two years Colonel David Humphreys, the American minister to Portugal, had been using that country's good offices to try to straighten out the troubles in the Mediterranean. Colonel Humphreys was a skilled negotiator and an extremely patient man. Swallowing insults and braving physical dangers by trying to visit the Barbary states, he managed to secure the cooperation of the French, who put pressure on the Deys, and brought forth a treaty of peace with Algiers, the most effective pirate state. For a sum of a million dollars, the captives were ransomed, the Dey promised to hold his corsairs in check, and a bright new future for American shipping seemed to be in the offing. Thus the enemies of preparedness in time of peace had their opportunity, and they struck in Congress, to bring about the halt of construction of the frigates on the ways.

In 1796 the opponents of militarism held that the American merchant navy should fend for itself, and not involve the federal government.

By the end of 1796 one of the most ardent supporters of neutrality was convinced that it was wrong. President George Washington abhorred the idea of interfering with any other nation, as much as he hated the thought that some other country might interfere with the United States. But his experience with the Barbary pirates was such that he concluded in his message to Congress that the most sincere neutrality was not enough to protect American citizens abroad from those who liked to prey upon the weak. It was his judgment, said the president, that America could never secure its own neutrality unless it built a naval force that was ready to protect the flag and all it meant, "from insult or aggression."

Just then, the president's words were extremely meaningful, for Britain and France were quarreling everywhere around the world; each power was trying to force the United States to actions, if not declarations of war, against the other. British ships wanted the American trade; they wanted the haven of American ports; they wanted Americans to deny the French enemy supplies and ammunition and haven. The French wanted the same. Each attacked the other in American waters, and the Americans had no way of enforcing their neutrality. At some point, it seemed certain, someone was going to light the torch of war.

Washington's words, then, convinced many who philosophically abhorred the concept of force that a naval establishment must represent, and a Navy Department was added to the federal government, with the ships and a handful of officers and men assigned.

Still, by the end of 1796 the future of the navy was clouded. Congress had originally appropriated a little under $700,000 for the ships that were in the process of being built. Unwilling to spend too much more, particularly in view of the expensive settlement with Algiers, Congress ordered the three most advanced frigates to be completed and the other three to be scrapped — and the hulls or materials sold to the highest bidders.

In 1797 American attitudes began to change considerably. Washington was no longer president, he had refused to stand for a third term, and had been succeeded by John Adams, with the very pro-French Thomas Jefferson as vice-president.

The French took the new American election to mean that the United States was leaning heavily toward their side, since both president and vice-president had spent much time in Paris. When this did not entirely prove to be the case, the French were annoyed. Affairs had already worsened. Angered by an American treaty of amicability with England, the French had refused to accept an American minister in 1796, just about the time of the American elections.

In 1797 they began harassing American shipping in a manner far more dangerous than the Algerian pirates had ever done. They kept

American vessels in French and French-colonial ports on various pretexts, tried to seize some, did seize others, and retained them until the cargoes rotted in almost every case. Diplomatic missions were unproductive. The revolution was on in France, and the revolutionaries were proving to be as arrogant as any king had been.

By the summer of 1797 even the most ardent neutrals began to have second thoughts, and the three frigates *Constitution*, *Constellation*, and *United States* received a new appropriation. They could be finished; more, the American people were becoming infuriated by French actions and the public was calling for the completion of the naval vessels. Some were loudly clamoring for war.

Then came September 1797.

*Constitution* was nearly ready for launching.

Earlier that year *United States* had been launched at Philadelphia, and *Constellation* at Baltimore. There had been problems, particularly with *United States*, for the ways were too steep, she had slid out fast, banged her false keel on the bottom of the river, and damaged the rudder brace so extensively that the vessel had to be hove down for repairs.

Learning from this, the builders of *Constitution* were determined to keep those ways more shallow, and they did so. On September 20 at Boston flags waved and banners dipped, and a huge crowd came to see the launching of this famous ship. The president was invited. The governor of Massachusetts came to the ceremony. The spectators were there by invitation only, and were kept back from the area, lest the sudden swell of water from the huge vessel overwhelm them.

Colonel Claghorn was ready that day, warning off pleasure craft from the bay side. All there waited for the height of the spring tide that was scheduled for the day. That would be the hour of launch.

The tide came, the chocks were knocked out, the speeches were made, the last block was removed, and the *Constitution* began to slide down toward the water.

She slid for twenty-seven feet — and stopped dead.

The colonel and Edmund Hartt the builder, and all those who had labored so long were red with mortification and upset. The embarrassment was almost too great to manage. The crowd was first sympathetic, then worried, and finally hooting. The colonel brought out his best mechanics. They applied screws to the system. Nothing happened.

They tried manpower and horsepower. Nothing happened.

The ways were too gentle of slope, not too steep.

*Constitution* was stuck.

That night of September 20, at the Haymarket Theater, the city held a hollow celebration. In

24

honor of the great ship the playwright John Hodgkinson had written a musical presentation called *The Launch, or Huzza for the Constitution.*

The show must go on, and it did that night, but to the further embarrassment of Colonel Claghorn and all those red-faced men who had participated in the building of the warship.

But the people of Boston took it in good humor. Disappointed or not, they trooped into the theater and there was a minimum of catcalls. Even the press refrained from taking the builders too fervently to task; *The Centinel* called on the public to accept the grave disappointment philosophically.

Meanwhile Colonel Claghorn and his men were working day and night to try to get *Constitution* out into the water. They managed to move her along another thirty feet, but this was the best they could do.

They were already worried about what effect the changing of the weights and pressures would have. Later some of those at the yard claimed that the *Constitution* was "hogged." That was true; she was hogged, or her keel slightly out of alignment, but the reason more frequently adduced for that condition was the immense size and weight of those oaken timbers. Several of the other frigates of the period were hogged as well; the deficiency was not corrected for a number of years.

But hogged or not, Colonel Claghorn and his men had to get that big ship into the water, and they did all they could. Sadly they came to the conclusion that the celebrants would have to go on home before it could be done, and come back if they wished at the highest tide of the month of October, when a new attempt would be made.

It was made.

The date was October 21.

Captain James Sever came for the occasion to smash a bottle of wine across the ship's bow and christen her, as all the optimists among the original crowd returned to see if the ship would move. The governor came and the mayor and many another bright light in the crown of Boston's citizenry.

The crowd began showing up around daylight, when Colonel Claghorn fired a gun, a prefixed signal that the ways were deemed proper, the tide was working right, and the launch was going to go on as scheduled.

All morning the people assembled, until 12:15, when Captain Sever stood up, picked up his wine bottle, and swung it heftily at the prow, above which stood the mighty figure of Hercules, carved and placed by the Skillings Brothers.

*Constitution* gave a little shudder as the last chock was moved, and then she began to slide. Down the ways she went, and the motion was described by a poetic newspaperman:

". . . She commenced a movement into the water with such steadiness, majesty and exactness as to fill almost every breast with sensations of joy and delight . . ."

There was but one minor difficulty, and that was the trouble of Captain Samuel Nicholson, the man chosen by Congress and the Navy Department to be the first captain of the *Constitution*.

For weeks Nicholson had been bedeviling the colonel and the builders about their slowness in bringing the ship to launch. He had been furious on the day of the failure, and had let his annoyance be known to all around him. So slurring were the words he had for the builder, the yard, the workmen — for all who had any part in the preparation of the frigate — that he had gained himself a hateful reputation at the shipyard.

On the night before the launch, Captain Nicholson let it be known that as soon as the ship was launched he proposed to run up the very first United States flag over her. It could not be done properly until she was christened and accepted by the government, but it certainly could be done the moment the launch was completed.

So the captain left absolute orders that no one else was to enjoy the privilege of the flag raising.

It did not quite work out that way.

Among those in the yard who had taken particular exception to the captain's harsh words about Boston shipbuilders and their workers was a caulker named Samuel Bentley, a hard-minded and long-remembering man. He had decided back in September that he would get back at the harsh-voiced captain and give him something to remember.

So when the frigate came thundering down the ways just after the clock struck 12:15 that day, there high above her taffrail, fixed to a spar, flew Old Glory, the new Old Glory, with fifteen stars to emblazon the honor of the states.

The captain had his comeuppance.

The captain was to have many another frustration before he ever got *Constitution* out to sea. Congress dithered as relations with France grew worse, and then better and then worse again. The number of officers was changed and changed another time. So was the number of men.

Finally, in 1798 as she was still in Boston harbor, the manning was set at twenty-two officers and 378 men. Captain Nicholson was the commander, and he had four lieutenants, plus a pair of lieutenants of marines, a sailing master (he was the navigator and real seaman), two master's mates, eight midshipmen, a purser, a surgeon, a chaplain, representatives of a dozen specialties from gunner to cooper, and three hundred fifty sailing and fighting men, not usually singled out by name, but the bone and sinew of the crew of the frigate *Constitution*. There were one hundred twenty able seamen, one hundred fifty ordinary seamen and thirty boys who were learning to sail, plus fifty marines who would fight the ship from the rigging and lead the boarding parties and chase enemies ashore.

The sailing trade was not well paid, and the

only man aboard her who could expect to have much to show for his service in a material way was the captain, who received a princely salary of $2,000 a year. The surgeon was next best paid at $800. The lieutenants received $786 each and the promise of being able to win their own captaincies in time, given a chance for valor. The chaplain, sailing master and purser were all paid about the same amount, indicating their place in the scale aboard a warship. Then came the surgeon's mate and the lieutenants of marines, then the boatswain, gunner, sailmaker, and carpenter — all earning more than the eight midshipmen, who received $432 each per year of service, and the possibility of promotion to lieutenant.

Way down below on the scale were the men, whose pay ranged from the nineteen dollars a month of a petty officer, to the eight dollars a month paid a boy.

In the spring of 1798 the manning of the *Constitution* was completed, and the officers and men came aboard to begin accustoming themselves to a new life. They were, in effect, the pioneers of a new navy, men and boys who would make the traditions and establish the honor of this new service of this new nation.

They had their uniforms, the blue and white and gold of the officers and the blue and sometimes white of the men, caps and blouses and trousers. For the most part in clement weather the men went barefoot; they had clothing for heavy weather and heavy clothing for winter, and each enlisted man had a space twenty-two inches wide and eight feet long in which to swing his hammock down on the mess deck near the waterline.

They had their food. Almost all of the regular ration was dried or salted. Salt beef and ship's bread and flour for duff alternated with saltpork and dried peas, rice, cheese, molasses, and vinegar. A Sunday's ration for example was 1.25 pounds of salt beef, 14 ounces of bread, half a pound of flour, a quarter pound of suet. What made it palatable was the spirit.

Every man had his ration of whiskey or rum, depending on what was purchased — a half-pint per day, month in and month out. When *Constitution* loaded up for sea, she boarded a hundred kegs of rum and whiskey, enough to issue twenty-eight gallons for every day. It was the biggest single item of expenditure aboard the ship.

Life aboard the *Constitution* was hard, for a sailing man's life was steaming or freezing, depending on the weather and the time of year. There was room for few fires aboard a wooden man of war. But as such ships went, *Constitution* was from the outset a happy ship, as were most American naval vessels. The British believed in a harsh discipline, of the kind that led to the famous mutiny on the *Bounty* and the mutiny in the fleet. British ships were notable for their foul food and water, and the cruelty of the disciplinary system that allowed a man to be flogged to death for a relatively minor crime. For the Americans, the maximum in lashes was limited to a dozen with the cat o' nine tails, and there was no imprisonment in a filthy cell below the waterline for minor offenses as there was for Jack Tar in his ship under the Union Jack.

As the officers trained the men of *Constitution* for sea, the French grew more contemptuous and trying in their activity. A French warship entered Charleston harbor and destroyed a British merchantman that was there on perfectly respectable business.

Other French ships roamed American waters, stopping and seizing U.S. vessels and sinking British ships or sending them off to Guadeloupe and other colonies, with prize crews aboard.

Soon Congress was approving the commissioning of privateers, and four squadrons of ships were assembled to cruise the West Indies and protect American trade while harrying that of the French. War was all but declared against the French government.

In June Captain Nicholson watched his crew train, and at the end of the month First Lieutenant Charles Russell declared they were ready to put to sea and fight for their country. So on July 2, 1798, with orders in the captain's hands, the *Constitution* dropped down from the inner Boston harbor to the roads, and cleared for sea some three weeks later, when all provisions were aboard, all the men ready, and the ship bound for action.

This was the shakedown.

At sea the men learned their gunnery under the conditions it would be practiced. Shooting a long gun or a carronade did not seem to be much of a problem — on land. But at sea firing a gun was a much different proposition.

The gun itself was a twenty-four pounder, which meant it had a bore of about 5.83 inches, and fired a solid shot that weighed about twenty-four pounds. It was about ten feet long, and it sat on one of Edmund Thayer's stout oaken gun carriages. The elevation of the gun was manipulated by the use of a handspike. The recoil was controlled by ropes and pulleys fastened to the bulkheads and the deck of the ship. The firing range was about six hundred yards, but at any range it took a skillful and lucky gunner to hit an enemy ship in the right place.

For the first month at sea, Captain Nicholson's men learned. They practiced seamanship — up and down the hempen rigging, in and out of the yards, swiftly on the ratlines. They practiced gunnery and damage control and boarding an enemy. Every one of those four hundred officers and men had a specific task to do under specific situations, and it was the first lieutenant's job to see that they got the tasks done in order and in the wink of time.

They ran the guns out; they fired their matches; they poured the powder and shot into the muzzle and rammed the mixture home, then ran the guns out again. They watched as the gunner's mate poured the powder into the gun's vent and "laid the train" — and then the whole guncrew watched again as the gunner sighted at their target, estimated the roll and pitch of the ship in the water, and as the gun moved into perfect firing position touched his match to the powder train, and the gun went off with a roar of anger and a cloud of fiery smoke. The gun was pulled back, turned, swabbed and cleaned, and more powder and shot rammed home, turned again, put through the black port, and was ready once again to fire.

The practice went on until August 21, when the captain, satisfied that *Constitution* was ready and would not disgrace her colors, put in at Newport for his orders. Captain Nicholson learned there that he was to head for Florida, to cruise from Cape Henry down to the tip of Florida in company of four small revenue cutters. They would be looking for French ships.

Two days later *Constitution* sailed, eager for action.

The ships cruised southward, without incident. The weeks became months, and the months moved onward until December came. Then the ship was taken from her unproductive duty and assigned to a squadron commanded by Commodore John Barry, one of the heroes of the Revolutionary War.

*Constitution* now was to go to the Windward Islands and cruise, looking for the French enemy, with a rendezvous point at Prince Rupert's Bay, where she was to meet the rest of the squadron.

So she went down, but again the results were negligible. There was a good reason for *Constitution*'s failure to come to grips with the French enemy — she was just too large a ship. The French did not send any of their ships to America, and *Constitution* never came into contact with one of their frigates. Instead, she was forever chasing fast privateers and sloops that could outrun her, and recognizing her, kept well out of the way. The fact was that the two most effective American ships in this whole "almost war" against France were a pair of fast schooners that managed to capture many enemy privateers.

The Navy Department realized that it was senseless to keep sending a frigate to do a schooner's job, and so in 1779 she was ordered back to Boston, and there Captain Nicholson was replaced in command by Commodore Silas Talbot. Talbot's revolutionary war career was as bright as Nicholson's had been, for while Nicholson had been a lieutenant under John Paul Jones, and then commanded the frigate *Deane*, Talbot had led a half-dozen different ships, fought with Lafayette, and even been imprisoned by the British during the war.

Nicholson, perhaps because of his arbitrary nature, seems to have been an unlucky man. Talbot was a much luckier one, at least at the time. Now in 1799 as Commodore, he was to take out one of the prides of the American navy. He was forty-eight years old and at the apex of his career. Serving under him was a young lieutenant named Isaac Hull, the most promising of the four lieutenants in the crew of *Constitution*. Hull had come to the navy from the merchant service, where he had been a bright and promising youngster. He had impressed Nicholson. Now he would impress Talbot.

After changing captains, *Constitution* set sail one August day in 1799 to return southward and prosecute the undeclared war against the French predators. She was to be the flagship of the San Domingo station, which would put her in the center of any action. She went down to cruise between Cayenne and the French major port of Guadeloupe, to keep the French under control and capture as many prizes as possible.

The prizes were disappointing. She was not fast enough to catch the swift little ships that plied this trade except under lucky circumstances, and they did not appear this time. The French did not send any frigates or ships of the line into her territory, and so there was no chance for a major engagement to prove her mettle.

After a few months Lieutenant Russell left the ship, and Talbot made Isaac Hull his first lieutenant, which meant that Hull was the executive officer of the ship, responsible for all her workings. Since Talbot was not only commander of *Constitution* but also commodore of the squadron, the responsibilities of Hull were more than that of the usual first lieutenant.

35

Hull was prepared for them. A stocky, smiling young officer, he was also the master of his trade, and without the heavy hand of discipline that marked the British ships of the period, he soon had *Constitution* a spit-and-polish ship that could be pointed to with pride by any American. The American people gave loving attention to the frigates of their navy in these years. It was a new navy, and the people welcomed it as a sign of national maturity.

The British welcomed the American frigates in quite another way. It was here in the Caribbean that his Majesty's Royal Naval officers first caught glimpse of the *Constitution*. With her heavy construction and tall rigging, she seemed over-equipped for the job she was designed to do, like a youngster who is too fat for his height and body structure. The younger British officers saw her and laughed: just like the upstart Yankees to try to build a better ship than their "masters" and fail to do it.

A handful of the more intelligent senior officers looked at Joshua Humphreys' creation and wondered. They were not so sure she was the blundering idiot of the sea that their young and foolhardy juniors claimed.

While cruising off San Domingo one day, *Constitution* spotted a ship of some size, and hoping it might be a French fighting vessel, Commodore Talbot overhauled the other ship, which then broke out the Union Jack. Antagonism to France had brought with it new friendliness to England for the moment, and Talbot soon ascertained that the British frigate before him was captained by an old acquaintance. Soon boats were exchanged, and the captain of the British frigate came aboard *Constitution* to pay a call on the commodore, who was senior. It was not just a duty chore; the captain was eager to inspect this new design.

Commodore Talbot was pleased to take the British officer on a tour of the warship. As usual, Lieutenant Hull and the crew had done well — there was nothing to be ashamed of this day, and the British captain declared himself much impressed.

There was just one thing, though, the British captain said.

Commodore Talbot looked his question.

It was doubtful if she would sail well on the wind — meaning to windward, which would necessitate tacking back and forth. He was willing to wager a cask of Madeira against whatever Commodore Talbot valued that the English frigate could beat *Constitution* in a sailing match.

Commodore Talbot was delighted. So was Lieutenant Hull, and the men of *Constitution* gave a great cheer at the news. There was to be a race.

In a way, Talbot was about to give away an important military secret, which was the extreme suitability of *Constitution* for just this task. For when Joshua Humphreys had sat at his drawing board, he had brought forth all his years of knowledge of the sea to put into this fighting ship design. From the French, no less, he had learned the trick of tapering the upper sides of the ship back in toward the center, to narrow the spar deck. Thus the gun deck below projected farther away from the keel. The result was to bring the rigging on the spar deck closer to the mast, and this meant the yards could be braced more sharply for sailing on the wind.

The British captain thought she looked awkward with that "tumble home," as they called the reverse angling of the sides at the top of the hull. With the British it was just the opposite. The main, or spar, deck was the broadest part of the ship.

Talbot was not fool enough to tell the Briton all this, but he did make an arrangement to meet his old acquaintance a few weeks later for the race. The British frigate was heading for port, for she had just come from a long voyage and needed a bottom scraping and paint.

It was arranged.

On the appointed day the vessels met, the British frigate as spotless as the day she was launched, and *Constitution* still new and bright. The captains dined together that night, and set the conditions for their race. On the firing of a gun at dawn they would begin.

Dawn came, and the harsh report of the signal gun sounded across the water. Isaac Hull had already given his preliminary orders, and now the men turned to, putting on the canvas that would enable them to beat to windward.

It was tack port and starboard, all day long, with the eagle-eyed young lieutenant watching every puff, ready to take advantage of the slightest shift as he worked for position.

Steadily, the British frigate dropped back, and by mid-afternoon she was so far back her individual sails were blurred. Hull did not let up — he estimated every change and figured every detail, even moving his crew from side to side of *Constitution* to take advantage of their weight in heeling. By dusk only the masts and sails of the British ship could be seen on the horizon.

Sunset ended the race. *Constitution* hove to then, and her big sails slacked and shivered in the wind as Commodore Talbot waited for the English captain to pay his debt. In an hour up came the Englishman, to dine aboard the victorious vessel, with his cask of Madeira under his arm, and a sad smile on his face.

The race had been an exciting event in what was really a dull life for the officers and men of *Constitution* this year. While the smaller frigate *Constellation* was out chasing and being chased, and winning victories over the *Insurgent* and the *Vengeance*, the bigger American frigate had no such luck.

Perhaps that is why on May 10, 1800, Commodore Talbot grew so impatient that he decided to force a bit of action.

The *Constitution* was on station, cruising off

San Domingo as ordered. It was dull, deadly work, stopping vessels for identification and intelligence, and then letting all neutrals go on about their business.

But from one neutral ship one day, Commodore Talbot learned that the French vessel *Sandwich* was loading coffee in the Spanish port of Porto Plata on the north side of San Domingo. He hastened around to the north side of the island. Soon, out of port came a sloop, which was stopped and boarded by a party from *Constitution*. The sloop was an American named *Sally*, and Talbot was about to let her go when he had an idea. Why not use this vessel to strike a blow against the French?

It was not as if *Sandwich* was just another merchant ship. She was a French privateer, and *Sally*'s captain felt lucky to have sneaked out of Porto Plata harbor before the French vessel was loaded and could give her chase.

Talbot had considered charging in with *Constitution*, engaging the Spanish fort with its three guns, and taking the French ship that way. He had given up that idea not because of any fear of the Spanish — did not the French invade neutral ports to take ships at will? — but because he was afraid he might damage *Constitution*. The *Sally* provided him with another route to glory.

Captain Carmick of the Marines and Lieutenant Amory were assigned to take *Sally* into port, with ninety armed men to attack the *Sandwich* and capture or burn the French ship.

Then Hull intervened. He insisted that he must be allowed to lead the expedition, and so great was the favor he had won with his commodore that Talbot could not refuse him. So Lieutenant Hull was put in overall charge of the escapade.

May 10 was the day. On the night before, the men were armed and instructed. They would go down into the hold of *Sally* and remain there quietly, while a half-dozen of their number, dressed carelessly as merchant seamen, worked the ship inshore under Lieutenant Hull's direction. Any suspicion at the return of the *Sally* would be allayed by her insignificant size and obvious civilian nature.

On that morning on the tide, Lieutenant Hull took his vessel into port and ran in under the Spanish guns, alongside the *Sandwich*. At a signal Hull led the seamen in boarding the French ship; sword in hand, he jumped across the space between them, even as Captain Carmick and Lieutenant Amory led the marines across on the other side, where they attacked the fort, spiked all its guns, and took control before the French and Spanish commanders of ship or fort could prepare themselves.

Not a man was lost. Not a man was wounded. It was the perfect example of the surprise attack.

In an hour they were out of the harbor again, this time with the *Sandwich* under American colors.

Commodore Talbot was immensely pleased.

His men had comported themselves with spirit and bravery, and they had done their task well. *Sandwich*, which mounted four six-pound guns and two nine-pounders, was a fine prize, and officers and men should share in prize money, not only from the beautifully copper-bottomed ship, which was held to be one of the fastest in the world, but from the loaded cargo of sugar and coffee.

But what a disaster it turned out to be for Commodore Talbot and the crew of the *Constitution*! When Commodore Talbot's letter describing the incident reached Washington, the Navy Department might have been expected to applaud, but that was not the case. The "war" with France was winding down, with growing irritation of Americans against the British for impressment of seamen from American vessels. Not many months before, the British had had the temerity to stop the American sloop of war *Baltimore* and take five sailors out of her. The quarrel with the French was not so important; there was no quarrel with the Spanish at all, and the State Department was very upset with the turn of events.

The result was that instead of being treated as heroes, the officers and men of the *Constitution* were slapped on the wrist. *Sandwich* was given back to the French. Even worse, all the prize money from the various minor captures of the cruise was also held back to pay off the damages claimed by the Spanish for the treatment of their military and the spiking of their expensive guns.

Glory they had. They got back to Boston in August 1800, to have the bad news and the good. The good news was that Commodore Talbot was not cashiered (as he might have been) but received a letter from Navy Secretary Stoddert praising him for all he had done. He took *Constitution* out again in November, and they stayed on the San Domingo station without much incident until the spring of 1801, when a treaty was made with France.

That treaty ended all need for frigates at sea, and brought up once again all the old arguments of the neutralists against the maintenance of a navy by the United States.

*Constitution* came home to Boston in March 1801. Commodore Talbot was ordered to other duty and went down to Washington. Lieutenant Hull supervised the payoff of the crew and took *Constitution* into Boston Navy Yard, where she was dismantled and laid up. Then Hull, too, went off. The lonely ship stayed still, the water lapping at her sides as she waited.

# CHAPTER TWO

## ON THE BARBARY COAST

The Barbary pirates were giving trouble again. Back before the turn of the century, the Americans thought they had matters all settled when they agreed to pay tribute to the Dey of Algiers. They built a fine frigate for him, the *Crescent*, and Americans sailed it for delivery in Algiers, carrying twenty-six barrels of dollars, many valuable gifts, and Consul General Richard O'Brien, who knew the Barbary Coast well as a former prisoner of the pirates.

Down the coast the Bashaw of neighboring Tripoli grew progressively more unhappy as he observed the tributes and obeisance the Americans paid to the Algerian ruler, his rival for power on the sea and for the good will of Constantinople. Two years after the delivery of the *Crescent* to Algiers, Tripoli demanded a frigate and tribute, and when it was refused the Bashaw became annoyed. The result was a declaration of war in the spring of 1801. At about the same time the Bey of Tunis took a similar position. The Americans were paying Algiers, so they should pay him too: they could begin with the delivery of forty new cannons, and ten thousand muskets and bayonets.

So war was renewed in the Mediterranean, although not much came of it immediately. Two American squadrons went to the Barbary Coast in those years, but the commanders were either not very vigorous or were bemused by confusing orders as to their obligations and duties.

That was before the coming of Preble.

Preble came in the fall of 1803, in *Constitution*. Captain Edward Preble was the finest type of American naval officer of that period — brave, audacious, and disciplined. He had been born in Portland, Maine, and he was forty-two years old, in the prime of his life it would seem. But it had been a hard life, beginning with service in a privateer when he was seventeen years old, service as a midshipman in the Massachusetts navy, and captivity under the British when his vessel was taken. He lived — or rather existed — aboard the infamous prison ship *Jersey* for several months before he was exchanged. That spell in the rotten ship broke his health and he never did recover, although his iron self-discipline kept most of his equals from knowing of his illness.

Like many another loyal American sailor, he was forced into the merchant marine at the end of the Revolutionary war because there was no navy, and he sailed around the world. But in 1798 he was appointed a lieutenant in the new navy, and he was made a commanding officer. Now, in the summer of 1803, he was chosen to do what two other captains had failed to do: take

*Constitution* and a squadron to the Mediterranean and tame the Barbary pirates.

When the news came that Preble was going to take her out, there was little trouble in securing a crew for *Constitution*. Naval service did have a problem — men enlisted to serve for a year only, which was no time at all considering the weeks it took to cross the Atlantic one way and then the other. But barring that difficulty, and the talk that men must enlist for two years, plenty of men wished to serve with this officer.

*Constitution* was also to be the flagship. The frigate *Philadelphia* under Captain William Bainbridge was to be the second ship. Then there were two brigs and three schooners to work inside along the coastline of the Barbary shore. It promised to be an exciting adventure, particularly to those who knew Preble.

On August 14 *Constitution* was ready, worked up, fully manned, provisioned, and she sailed, bearing with her Tobias Lear, Consul General of the United States, to the Barbary powers. The American government in Washington was cautious: if the pirates wanted peace they could have it, and if they wanted war, Preble would give them a taste of gunpowder.

The ships of the squadron were scattered, but they were instructed to meet Preble at Gibraltar that autumn, and then begin enforcing the naval rights of American citizens under the rules of the sea and various treaties.

Early in September, after a pleasant voyage, *Constitution* was nearing Gibraltar, expecting to end her voyage after twenty-nine days from Boston. Sailing to the British fortress was not quite what an American naval man would have ordered, but officially the countries were friendly. Actually the friction between the American men of the sea and the English navy was growing more intense every month of every year.

The harsh service under the Royal Ensign caused many a British tar to desert to other services. In these days perhaps half the American naval service on the enlisted level was manned by foreigners of various nationalities, and to be truthful a large number of "American" sailors were Scots and Irish and Englishmen. So there was justice on both sides; it was the nicety and lack of it that made for conflict. The British continued to stop American vessels and impress American seamen, usually claiming that these "impressed" men were actually deserters from the service. The Americans might or might not know the true origins of the men, but they resented the brutal and humiliating action every time. And because the British naval vessels generally overpowered the American ships, there was no fight, and the British officers tended to think of the Americans as cowards or second-class navy men.

So the conflict grew.

Well aware of this state of affairs as he approached European waters, Preble was ready.

One dark night, just a few hours from Gibraltar, the *Constitution* was sailing along under heavy canvas, trying to take advantage of very light winds. Suddenly the lookouts hailed that another vessel was nearby, and she seemed to be rigged as a ship of war.

Preble brought the crew to quarters, his officers speaking quietly. She might be anything — he could well remember the depredations of the Algerians outside the gates of Hercules in years past.

He stood on his bridge. They came upon the other ship, her form limned against the dark horizon.

"What ship is that?" hailed the commodore.

"What ship is that?" came the answering hail from across the water.

"United States frigate *Constitution*," replied Commodore Preble, courteously. "What ship is that?"

"What ship is that?" came the response mockingly.

Preble's patience came to an abrupt end. He seized the speaking trumpet, to be sure he was well understood, and he shouted out, clear and slow.

"I am now going to hail you for the last time. If a prompt answer is not returned, I will fire a shot into you."

"If you fire a shot, I will return a broadside," came the answer.

"What ship is that?" shouted Preble.

"This is his Britannic Majesty's ship *Donnegal*, eighty-four guns, Sir Richard Strahan, an English commodore. Send your boat on board."

Preble turned scarlet at the insult. He leaped high up on the bulwarks of his flagship and answered as loudly and clearly as he could.

"This is the United States ship *Constitution*, forty-four guns, Edward Preble, an American commodore who will be damned before he sends his boat on board of any vessel."

And jumping down, he turned to First Lieutenant Thomas Robinson.

"Blow your matches, boys," he said.

He was ready to fire off a broadside on a moment's notice.

The other captain seemed to have understood, finally, that he had gone too far. For in a few minutes the creak of oars could be heard across the water, and soon a boat arrived, and an officer announced sheepishly that he came from the British frigate *Maidstone*.

There were apologies. The British vessel had not seen the American ship until after Preble had first hailed, and then the captain had worried. For what if she was a Frenchman — he had to have time to bring his crew to general quarters, get them at their guns and be ready to fight. That was the occasion for the apparent rudeness.

Preble could certainly understand that reasoning. Any good fighting captain would have done the same — there was no occasion to mention the lack of discipline or watchfulness that had allowed the American ship to creep up so closely that had she been truly a Frenchman she could have blown the *Maidstone* clean out of the water before the British could fire a shot.

So the apology was accepted and the ships soon separated, the British going away with a slightly altered feeling toward at least one of those American captains. This one had proved to be quite a fire eater.

The squadron assembled, the ships straggling in as best they could from their various positions around the Mediterranean. Preble assembled his captains; he was displeased. Bainbridge, the eldest of them, was twenty-nine years old, and the rest were even younger. Lieutenant Isaac Hull now had his own ship, the brig *Argus*. Lieutenant Charles Stewart had the *Siren*; Lieutenant John Smith had the schooner *Vixen*; Lieutenant Richard Somers had the schooner *Nautilus*; and Lieutenant Stephen Decatur had the schooner *Enterprise*. The ships were perfectly fine, picked for their particular performance in the shoal waters that were to be fished for pirates. But those youngsters! Preble grumbled that the navy was doing him wrong. "They sent me a gang of boys," he complained to Consul Lear.

But as a good sailor and officer, Preble set out with the forces available to him to put down the Barbary pirates and make the Mediterranean safe for American shipping.

The Secretary of the Navy had been quite honest with Preble when he gave him the command. He was not getting enough men or enough ships or guns, and he was being asked to do a job that was very nearly impossible under the circumstances. But that was the way it had been with the American forces from the beginning of the revolution. Preble was used to it. Just about everything was wrong — the supply system, the manning system, and the unavailability of funds. But Preble was determined to get along.

His first problem was desertion. At one point the American government was paying so much less than a man could earn in the merchant service that native Americans would not enlist. "I do not believe I have more than twenty native Americans aboard," Preble wrote home gloomily one day. That was possible — the year was 1803 and the American republic was just twenty years old. But of course that was not the basic reason for the problem; the manning system was dreadful. There were so many desertions of the Americans at Gibraltar and Malta that within a few weeks Preble quit these ports for supply and set up his base of operations at Syracuse in the Two Sicilies. This at least had the apparent advantage of putting him in neutral territory between the British and French, who were struggling for the Mediterranean. Preble did not want to get caught up in the wars between these powers while doing his job for America.

Blockade was the task ahead of the squadron. To achieve it, *Philadelphia* was sent to stand off

Tripoli and keep shipping from entering or leaving the port. The fourteen-gun schooner *Vixen* accompanied her. *Vixen* was to be like a pilot fish for a shark, nosing into shallows and hidden places and warning the bigger ship when danger threatened. *Constitution* moved over to Tangier for a while, with *Nautilus* and the frigate *John Adams*. The flagship then cruised between Gibraltar and Tangier and off the coast of Morocco.

Preble wanted to make a show of force there, because the Emperor of Morocco had been fishing in dangerous waters. There was reason to believe he had slipped in conforming to his treaty with America and was working with the openly inimical Tripoli pirates. The plan worked — in a matter of weeks the emperor signed a new treaty with the Americans. There would be no more tributes here, but mutual concessions about trade and protection. For some days during the negotiations, the men of *Constitution* had slept at their guns in Tangier harbor. But it came out peacefully, and in October, 1803, it could be said that Morocco was stable and pacified, and Preble could move on to other tasks.

His next move was back to Gibraltar, where he found the pickings in supply most unusually thin. The British needed their materials for their own vessels, and were not inclined to give up such vital parts as anchors and chain to a neutral, no matter the relationship. So, soon, Preble took *Constitution* over to Cadiz for anchor and chain and fresh water to fill his casks, since Gibraltar depended on a rain supply that was most uneven. That done, just to check up on the Emperor of Morocco, he dropped back by Tangier, ready to talk or fight. There was no need to fight, the consul assured him that the emperor was living up to the spirit and letter of the new treaty, and the sight of the *Constitution* in harbor, with all those guns bristling from the ports on the gundeck, did not do a bit of harm.

At Gibraltar again, the commodore had word, through the brig *Argus,* of affairs to the east. He sat down at the desk in his cabin in *Constitution* and wrote a draft of a letter to the various American ministers and consuls around Europe. Tripoli's Bashaw had chopped down the pole that flew Old Glory above the American consulate in Tripoli, and the answer was war. Tripoli was now in a state of siege, the commodore warned, and let the various ministers and consuls so advise the shipping owners of Europe. Any vessels that tried to put in at the pirate port were liable to seizure and forfeit to the Americans.

There was a certain amount of command housekeeping to be done. Preble had to deliver Colonel Lear to Algiers, which he did, and then he headed for Syracuse, which was to be the base.

En route he met the British ship *Amazon* off the coast of Sardinia, and the captains got together for a talk.

Disaster!

Here Commodore Preble learned that just three weeks before the *Philadelphia* had grounded on a rock near Tripoli, and that Captain Bainbridge and his entire crew had been captured when she would not come off the rock.

Thus in one day, Preble had lost a third of his seapower, and he was enjoined by Washington to put an end to the depredations of the Bashaw.

There was worse news, which Preble picked up at Malta where he stopped on his way to Syracuse. Not only had *Philadelphia* been lost to him, but the envious Bashaw had indeed secured the frigate he coveted. His admiral, a Scotchman by birth, had gone out at high tide and floated the *Philadelphia* off her reef and brought her into Tripoli harbor, where she was being repaired and would undoubtedly be used by the pirates to challenge the Americans at sea.

Preble, then, faced deep trouble.

He had to assign one of his vessels to guard the straits at Gibraltar, and that left him the *Constitution* and four small vessels, each captained by a "boy." Winter was coming, with the storms and heavy seas that characterized the North African coast. So severe were they that *Vixen*, the little schooner assigned earlier to Bainbridge's command, took thirty days getting, from Malta, the 130 miles to Syracuse, and only because of storms.

It threatened to be a long war.

In the middle of December, Commodore Preble took *Constitution* out of Syracuse harbor and headed for Tripoli on a mission of discovery and observation; he was accompanied by Lieutenant Smith's *Vixen* and Lieutenant Decatur's *Enterprise*. Off Tripoli, Decatur managed by ruse to capture a Tripolitan ketch, the *Mastico*, and from the officers and crew they learned that the Bashaw had nineteen gunboats in Tripoli harbor, that the castle and the harbor were heavily fortified, and that the crew of the *Philadelphia* was now at work building even more sturdy fortifications for the enemy. It was disturbing news, made palatable only by the capture, and by a plan worked out by Preble and Lieutenant Decatur.

Sailing back to Syracuse, the *Mastico* in tow, Preble fumed about the capture of *Philadelphia*. He did not blame Bainbridge, that man was suffering in the Bashaw's prison, and the English indicated that Bainbridge was victim of poor charts and bad luck. But blame or not, Preble squirmed at the thought of those pirates treading the decks of an American warship, and he determined that he would put an end to it, even if it meant destroying a ship of his own nation.

And so the plan was turning over in his mind.

While the commodore was thinking about it, his "boys" began to ask for action posts. Stephen Decatur suggested that he take *Enterprise* in and capture *Philadelphia* by boarding and then sailing her out. The idea was sweet in Preble's ears, but impractical. He did not know nor could he learn the condition in which the rigging and canvas of *Philadelphia* would be found on capture.

Lieutenant Stewart offered to go in and cut her out using the *Siren*. Again, the plan was too dangerous and depended on factors the Americans could not possibly know.

But what about using the *Mastico* — a Tripolitan ship which was sure to be recognized by the Bashaw's men and offer no suspicion as she came sailing in? Man her with Americans, let them sail up to *Philadelphia*, board and burn her, and then sail out if they could. God help them if they could not!

And that plan, worked out with Lieutenant Decatur, was the one settled upon.

The weather precluded action in the rest of December or in January, but on February 2, 1804, Decatur set out with a volunteer crew of men and officers that included five midshipmen from *Constitution*. If Preble could not have the job himself, at least the flagship would share the glory.

They reached Tripoli on February 6, and were in sight of their objective, when a dreadful gale sprang up, and drove them off to the east in a sea that frothed and churned for six long days and six longer nights. *Mastico* was *Mastico* no longer, but had been christened *Intrepid* when she was enlisted under the Stars and Stripes. Had she not been manned by an intrepid crew, she might have foundered in the storm, but Decatur saved her, and on the seventh day she was just outside the harbor of Tripoli. As the weather calmed she sailed into port bravely, as though she was indeed still *Mastico*, returning from the mission on which she had been sent, to procure black slaves for the Bashaw's retinue.

The story of Decatur's adventure is one of the great tales of the sea. He and a Maltese pilot lounged on deck with a handful of seamen dressed in Moorish style, while the volunteers lay in the hold with their pistols and cutlasses.

In they sailed, devil may care, and when they came up to the *Philadelphia*, they were hailed by the watchman of the ship. The pilot, Salvatore Catalano, replied that they were traders who had lost their anchor in the storm and asked permission to tie up to the *Philadelphia* overnight. The storm had been fierce; the watchman was tired; and for weeks no signs of the Americans had been seen. What was to be lost? The watchman gave permission; the officer of the deck gave permission; and the Tripolitan pirates even helped the men in the boat tie up the ketch for the night.

Soon, the men were emerging from their hiding place. Decatur had his seamen pull the ketch right up against the side of *Philadelphia* and then shouted the order that sent them boarding, weapons in hand, and selected men carrying materials to fire the ship. It was all worked out. One midshipman went aft, one below, one to the mainmast — every man had his place, and Decatur led them in. In five minutes they were aboard and had the deck, while the shout came from the after part of the ship.

"Americanos! Americanos!"

And, too late, the Tripolitan pirates tried to rally and drive the invaders off.

Ten minutes more went by, and the fires were lit, and then another five minutes and the frigate was blazing redly at half a dozen spots. The fires aft were quickly out of control, and it was apparent that the ship would burn.

The heat on deck was growing intolerable, and the men had their escape to make in the darkness and the confusion. Decatur gave a signal, and they headed back for the *Mastico*, cut her loose, and began rowing as hard as they could manage to clear the ship.

The pirates shrieked and waved their fists as the Americans rowed. Then came shots. At first Decatur believed the enemy had recovered and was shooting at the ketch. Worse luck! But then he saw — the shots came from the *Philadelphia*; her loaded guns were firing as the flames reached them and destroyed their carriages and the decks beneath them. What hard luck it would be if the Americans were destroyed by their own guns.

Soon these were not the only shots; the Tripolitans found their gunboats, and the shore batteries began to range on the little ketch as she struggled for the mouth of the harbor.

Behind, the town was alight with gunfire and flame. *Philadelphia*'s fires were licking at the foretop yards, and occasionally a hit of powder would go off, sending up a cloud of smoke.

Eventually they reached the mouth of the harbor and the safety of the open sea. There they were rejoined by Lieutenant Stewart in the brig *Siren*. Together the ships traveled back to Syracuse without incident. They arrived on Sunday morning, February 19, in winds so slight that Preble sent the boats of the *Constitution* out to tow the ships into harbor. One boat brought back the word of the triumph, and so, when the *Siren* and the *Intrepid* moved inside the mole and passed through the squadron, the men of the ships were at the rail to give them three cheers as they passed.

Preble was a fine and generous commander, and when Lieutenant Decatur came to the cabin of the *Constitution* and told the tale of his daring action, the commodore sat down forthwith and wrote to the Secretary of the Navy, recommending promotion and other rewards. In America, when the news arrived, it electrified the country, for Americans needed evidence that their navy had power on the seas. Overnight Decatur became a national hero. He received a sword from Congress, and he was promoted, to become the youngest captain in the United States Navy.

That news was months in returning to Syracuse. In the interim, Preble put Decatur in command of a number of smaller vessels and used his hero well, as he used all those "boys" whose presence he had lamented in the beginning. As for *Constitution*, she was forever in motion that spring and summer of 1804. She sailed from Syracuse on March 1 and made nineteen stops between that date and the first of July, as Commodore Preble patrolled his Barbary ports and ascertained what was happening. It was the best way for a commander to know in these days before wireless, when dispatch vessels could become becalmed or delayed at sea for weeks on end. It was a measure of Preble's excellence that he spent so much time at sea; another commander might have chosen to relax in the relative luxury of Syracuse and let his younger officers take the brunt of action.

The burning of the *Philadelphia* should have cooled down the warlike ardors of the Bashaw of Tripoli. Toward the end of March, Commodore Preble took *Constitution* there to discover the state of mind of the enemy. Although the people were restless, the Bashaw was stubborn, and no progress was made toward freeing the American captives. All Preble could do was send ashore some mail and provisions for the imprisoned men. He did secure some information because he and Bainbridge were corresponding in a secret code; but all he learned was that the Bashaw was not yet brought to his knees. Preble would have to go away and think awhile on his next move to bring that ruler to terms.

The Mediterranean was stormy and rough, and Preble was sick half the time during the voyage. His lungs had been affected by the cold harshness of life in the prison ship during the revolution. He coughed and worked and worried; not for a moment did he lose sight of his objective, which was to bring all the Barbary pirates to their knees and secure promise of safety for American trade.

In April he called in at Tunis, to be sure the Bey was keeping his promises, and was reassured that all was well. At the end of the month, Lieutenant Stewart managed to capture a Tripolitan brig with some military stores. That was a minor victory for the squadron, but not enough to satisfy Preble. It was necessary that the Bashaw be taught an even harsher lesson than the burning of his "new frigate" had done. An attack was indicated.

The problem of launching an attack lay in the shortage of ships and men allocated by Washington to the squadron. The crew of *Constitution* had very nearly mutinied over the question of enlistments; many of them were short-timers, whose enlistments had run out or were running out, and when they learned that they were not going home that spring, they were furious. Preble managed to resolve the problem, but just barely. Still, when some were persuaded to re-enlist, and others were shipped home in supply vessels, the problem of manning the flagship remained. He could not spare men to man small boats, if he had had small boats with which to attack Tripoli inside the rocks and jetties of the harbor.

Whatever the problems, the Secretary of the Navy made it quite clear that Preble was expected to solve them himself, with a minimum of expenditure, and a maximum of verve. It was quite an order.

Commodore Preble saw one way. He went to Naples, the capital of the Two Sicilies, and there he persuaded the King and his ministers to lend the Americans six gunboats and two mortar boats to stage an attack on Tripoli. The king was of two minds; a French faction at the court was not helpful to the American cause. But in the end, Preble secured his small craft, and the right to enlist some Sicilians in the struggle. That was most important in view of his manpower problems.

Sometimes it seemed that the Commodore and his flagship could never settle down to one task. Hardly had he secured the small gunboats and mortar boats than he learned a number of Tunisian warships had put to sea, and he had to drop everything and rush to Tunis to make sure that they were not going out to attack Americans. Satisfied that they were not, he returned to his preparations for the assault on Tripoli. On July 14, the men of *Constitution* made sail and took gun vessels and mortar ships in tow, as did the other ships of the squadron. They moved out, toward Tripoli and action once more.

Had Preble been still in possession of *Philadelphia* or another frigate the odds would have been better for this assault, for as it was, he was outgunned by the Bashaw and far outmanned. *Constitution* was rated as a forty-four-gun frigate.

She carried thirty long twenty-four-pounders on the gun deck, six long twenty-four-pounders on the gangways, and eight thirty-two pounders (carronades) on the forecastle and quarter deck. The other ships, between them, mounted seventy guns of various sizes, the gunboats were each equipped with a single twenty-four-pounder in the bow, and the bomb ketches carried a single brass mortar of thirteen inches in diameter, that threw a big explosive shot, but not very accurately. The whole squadron amounted to a thousand officers and men.

As for the Bashaw, he had twenty-five thousand men under arms, and his Scotch admiral had trained a strong force of pirate sailors who had for years scourged the seas about them and earned a fierce reputation as fighters. The harbor installations held 119 guns, and then there were the warships. The Bashaw owned nineteen gunboats, two galleys, two schooners and a brig, and all of them were well armed and manned by gunners who could shoot accurately.

Some commanders would not have chanced an action under these conditions. That was one of the reasons Preble was here. Commodore Morris had been in the Mediterranean for months with a squadron and never got into a fight at all. He was suspended, and Preble chosen because the Secretary of the Navy believed he would fight.

He did. Between July 25 and September 4, *Constitution* and the squadron stood off Tripoli most of the time and made four attacks against the city and its forts.

Standing offshore on the evening before the first attack, *Constitution* was a mother hen, feeding her young. The smaller vessels came to her that evening and filled their water casks, for they carried only a week's supply, and no one expected the affair to be over in a day or two. They were ready.

Next day began with northeast breezes, not the best, but not impossible, and they moved down on the enemy, to anchor about two and a half miles off the town. The smaller ships planned then to tow the gunboats inshore, for the attack, while *Constitution* covered them with her broadside. But by afternoon, when the ships were ready, the breezes had developed into a northeast gale, and the whole squadron was driven to sea for several days. The gale raged, *Constitution* pitched and tossed until the mess decks were soaked and the men miserable in the storm. The men reefed the sails, and double reefed them. And yet so powerful was the African wind that in one squally moment a gust ripped open her foresail and main topsail as though they were bits of paper and not stout canvas.

For two more days the storm continued, then began to abate, so that on August 3 Preble could again move to the attack. On the afternoon of the next day, the whole squadron moved in to point-blank range of Tripoli, and the firing began.

They stood just outside the barrier reef that made Tripoli so comfortable a port for the pirate ships.

When the Tripolitan admiral saw them coming, he moved to action. He sent his nineteen gunboats out in three divisions contemptuous of the Americans, for he was convinced by the capture of the *Philadelphia* and the previous actions of Commodore Morris, that American naval men were cowards who would not fight.

Commodore Preble had made sure they *would* fight. He sent the gunboats inside the reef in two divisions, one commanded by Lieutenant Somers and the other by Decatur.

How they did fight! Each American gunboat moved down on an enemy, firing as it came. But that was not the American object — soon the Yankees were boarding the Tripolitan vessels, hacking and shooting as they came, and inside an hour three of the Tripolitan boats were captured, and so were fifty-two prisoners, to swell the ranks of those to be exchanged for the Americans inside the Bashaw's dungeons.

One action totally infuriated the Americans, and made sure the Tripolitan pirates could afterward ask for little quarter. Decatur's younger brother, James, was aboard one of the American gunboats; he attacked a pirate boat, and the captain surrendered. Then, when young Decatur went to board and take possession, the captain treacherously murdered him.

Stephen Decatur had returned to the *Constitu-*

*tion* with a prize, and he was on the spar deck when the word came of the manner of death of his brother. He hastened over the side, into his gunboat, found the killer in his craft, attacked, killed his brother's murderer, and came back filled with grief to report. That was the kind of fighting the Americans did in Tripoli harbor that day.

As the attack ended, it was apparent that it had been satisfactory. Three boats were captured. Three were sunk in the harbor, and three more had been hit. The Bashaw had lost half the fighting men aboard the gunboat force; some of the batteries were knocked out by the shot of *Constitution*, and a minaret had fallen in the battle. The people ashore were impressed, some were already leaving the town for the countryside, where they hoped to be saved. For *Constitution*'s guns that day had fired 262 round shot, and scores of shots of canister, grape, and the vicious double heads, which consisted of a pair of shots chained together to do the most damage to soldiers and guns. As for the frigate's damage, she had been struck only a handful of times, most serious was one shot that damaged her mainmast. The others went through the sails or tore the hempen rigging. There was nothing wrong that could not be put to rights, although the mainmast would be a problem until they reached port once again and it could be replaced.

Although it was a victory, the anxious Preble

had hoped for much more. Stephen Decatur was the hero of the day once again, and though bowed down with the grief of his brother's death, he came to Preble at the end of the action.

"Well, Commodore," he said, "I have brought you out three of the gunboats."

Preble turned on his favorite lieutenant.

"Aye, sir, why did you not bring me out more?"

And in a rage, he marched into his cabin and shut the door.

But in a few moments the commodore was in control of himself, and he sent for Decatur and apologized to the younger man. It was not the fault of Preble's lieutenants if the task given him was more difficult than anyone had imagined.

That night, once young Decatur and the other dead were buried with military honors, the squadron celebrated the victory. The casualties had been surprisingly light for the damage inflicted. But Preble had little time for celebration. The responsibility hung heavy on him, and already he was planning and worrying about how to punish the city, retrieve the captives, and secure the peace of the area.

For three days he supervised the refitting and readiness for another attack. At least they had three more gunboats, the Tripolitan vessels captured in the first fight.

Preble then carried out an act of mercy. Fourteen of the captured pirates were severely injured, and he feared they might die on his hands.

He had no time to take them away to hospital, nor any ships that could be diverted from the war for the purpose. When a French vessel came along, heading for the harbor, since France was not at war with Tripoli, Preble stopped the ship and put the fourteen men aboard her, sending them in so the Bashaw's doctors might try to save their lives.

Such tenderness was almost incomprehensible to the Bashaw and his officers, for theirs was a fierce world in which the infidel was slaughtered or enslaved. The Bashaw decided on what for him was an act of great compassion. He sent word with the French ship that he was disposed to friendliness. The Americans might even send in a flag of truce.

Preble grimaced when he learned this news. The Bashaw was not cowed yet; if he wanted to hoist a white flag, the Americans would accept the surrender.

No white flag showed above the fort next day, so the attack was renewed.

The wind was all wrong for *Constitution*, she could not fight with the danger of dragging down and going aground outside the town, where she would become a sitting target. So Preble took her offshore, and cruised back and forth, while the smaller vessels did the work on this day, August 7.

As the sun came up, the preparations began. The gunboats and the bomb ketches moved into position and began firing. In all, they fired nearly

550 shots that day, into the forts, the guns, the boats and ships, and into the town. The people were in panic, and began streaming out of Tripoli in fear that the Americans were going to take the town at any moment.

But it was not all positive victory. A Tripolitan shot exploded the magazine of Lieutenant Caldwell's boat, and he and nine other men were killed. There were other casualties, and many of the gunboats and ketches were hard hit before the squadron hauled off at six o'clock in the evening.

Next day the frigate *John Adams* appeared on the scene, and for a brief moment, Commodore Preble hoped that he might have another twenty-eight guns to throw against Tripoli. One more attack might finish the work. But the reasoning of the Navy Department was strange. *John Adams* had been sent abroad to a war without her guns. They were coming in the supply train. She was no more use than a big merchant ship, except that her men could augment the slender force of the squadron, and they did. There was another advantage: the Bashaw did not know *John Adams'* true condition. That ruler must have been impressed, for before another attack could be made, the Bashaw sent a messenger to the French consul who hoisted a white flag and then Preble sent in a boat under flag of truce. Negotiations began for the ransom of the captives of *Philadelphia*. Preble offered $100,000. The

Bashaw refused. The negotiations ended and on August 24, Preble and the squadron once again attacked the city of Tripoli with all the force they could muster.

This was a night attack; the little boats were towed in close under cover of darkness and began firing at two o'clock in the morning. They blew up buildings and damaged the castle and knocked out guns. One shot went through the wall of the prison where Captain Bainbridge was kept, struck the bed in which he was sleeping, and still did not injure him!

But the town was much hurt by this time, and the constant repetition of attack was wearing on the people. The Bashaw's prestige was reduced, and even more so on the night of August 28, when *Constitution* moved in against the city and opened a heavy fire. Preble risked his flagship this day; she came in within four hundred yards of the sharp rocks, under heavy fire of the batteries. She fired three hundred round shot, and grape and canister, into the forts and the town. The gunboats and the other vessels came in as *Constitution* hauled out, and they did more damage, sinking ships and putting holes in the walls and the buildings.

When it was over, the first lieutenant gave Commodore Preble a rundown on *Constitution*. She had been hurt this time, her rigging was cut up and the crew examining her hull picked several rounds of grape shot out of her sides. But not a man was injured — that remarkable fact was trumpeted through the fleet and added to the brave reputation the flagship had already gained.

Early in September *Constitution* lay idly at anchor off Tripoli, as Preble's men moved water and stores from the ships that had accompanied *John Adams* on the voyage. Fresh meat and dry provisions — really not fresh, but more freshly salted than the stores that had come over a year before, or anything they had procured at Gibraltar or at Malta recently.

The weather was fine, and so Preble determined on another attack on September 3. It was carried out at long range, for the Tripolitan galleys and gunboats had moved up the harbor to the windward of the entrance — which made it very difficult for *Constitution*. But the ships attacked town and batteries again, as effectively as ever. They fired for an hour and a half until the wind swung around to endanger the flagship if she stayed. Then they all pulled out, leaving behind a number of disabled galleys and gunboats, and more destroyed guns in the forts, more holed buildings in the town.

What was needed was some brave act like Decatur's burning of the *Philadelphia*. Lieutenant Richard Somers came up with a plan. He wanted to take that ketch *Intrepid* into the harbor, set up as a fireship, and then to fire her and let her run about destroying the Bashaw's ships. Preble assented, and a hundred barrels of powder were loaded aboard the ketch; powder and shells were arranged, and a fuse set for fifteen minutes was led to a box filled with burnable material. Somers took her in, accompanied by a pair of boats in tow, so that he and his brave crew could escape in those fifteen minutes after they fired the *Intrepid.*

In they went, Somers and Lieutenants Henry Wadsworth and Joseph Israel, along with ten men, six of them seamen from the *Constitution.* Both Henry Wadsworth and Joseph Israel had also come from the flagship, where they had originally joined as midshipmen at the beginning of the cruise.

It was a night entrance. By eight o'clock they were under sail and standing toward the western entrance to the harbor. Last seen, they were a hundred yards off the mole, sails set, and heading inward in the darkness.

They must have been discovered. For suddenly the harbor was lit up with the flashes of guns from the shore. Preble had a feeling of despair, and later as he traced out what had occurred, he came to believe that Somers and his men had been discovered by an enemy gunboat, and challenged.

But they were not taken. Instead, there came an extremely bright light, and then a thunderous roar — and all the American squadron outside knew then that the *Intrepid* had blown up. Preble was sure too that he knew why: young Somers had sworn that he would never be taken alive, and if the enemy had approached him, as Preble believed, then Somers had put a match to the magazine and blown them all out of existence.

As if to lend credence to the commodore's belief, a search next morning discovered that the largest Tripolitan gunboat of all was missing, and several of the others seemed to be hardly afloat.

Tripoli *was* impressed. The word was now common in the streets that the Americans were devils in a fight, not the sheep they had been made out to be. Half the brave seamen of the Bashaw bore wounds or shock from the experiences they had in fighting Preble and his men. The town was a shambles, from the constant bombardments of *Constitution* and the smaller vessels. The Bashaw hid in the innermost recesses of his castle, most of his officials stayed in with him, and as for the people, they had deserted the town and there was no business being transacted there in the fall of 1804.

Preble had word from letters brought by the *John Adams* that he was to be superseded. Commodore Samuel Barron was coming to the area, and since he was senior to Preble, he would be the commodore of the squadron. So Preble sent the smaller vessels away for supplies and remained on station outside Tripoli to await the coming of Barron.

On September 10 frigates *President* and *Constellation* arrived, and Barron took command. But Preble was still captain of *Constitution* and there was one more task for him, one vital to the defeat of Tripoli. One day while cruising, the *Constitution* came upon a pair of blockade runners, and took them, then learned that they were laden with grain for the blockaded city. There had seldom been a more fortuitous capture.

The capture left Tripoli very near starvation.

Barron, when he and Preble met, was at some pains to inform the man he was superseding that Congress had not turned against Preble, nor had the Navy Department. As was usual with government, the coming of Barron and the larger squadron was a direct reaction to the capture of the *Philadelphia*. No one in Washington even suspected that Preble would be able to do what he had done with a single frigate, a handful of small vessels, and a batch of "boys."

In reality, the war was over, and Preble had won it; he had wiped out the disgrace of the *Philadelphia*, punished the Bashaw and Tripoli unmercifully, shaken the very throne, brought unwilling respect for American might to every corner of the Mediterranean.

Now Preble was to go home. *Constitution* took him to Malta, where he took over the *John Adams*. By this time, Stephen Decatur's promotion to captain had come through, and he was given command of *Constitution*. He was only to keep that command for about two weeks, when Captain John Rodgers came up in *Congress*. The latter was the smaller ship, and Rodgers was the senior captain, so Rodgers took over *Constitution* that November.

"*Connie*" had been at sea a long time without a refit. She needed a new suit of sails, cables, and a new bowsprit to replace damage done by the Barbary pirates in all those fights. Remarkably, although she was eighty men short in her crew that November, only one man had been removed from the ship because of injury; a single Marine suffered a shattered arm in the first attack on the Tripolitan capital. After that, not a man on her decks was hurt.

*Constitution* went to Lisbon that winter, then, and stayed there for several weeks, while she was cleaned and polished and took on what was needed for her good service. She came back in February to join the squadron, stopping off at Tangier to impress the Moroccans again that the Americans were about. When *Constitution* arrived off Tripoli once more in March, 1805, she joined the blockade, and it was not long before Captain Rodgers led her in capture of a Tripolitan privateer that was making for its home base, having taken a pair of Neapolitan prizes. So much the better — "*Connie*" was paying back the King of the Two Sicilies for lending Preble the gunboats and the mortar ketches. It was fair treatment.

In that spring of 1805, Commodore Barron fell ill and had to leave the squadron, so Rodgers became the commodore, and once again *Constitution* was the flagship.

The months of successful blockade told. In the spring many different efforts paid off, most of them begun by Preble. For one thing, the Bashaw knew about the fighting qualities of Americans. For another, Preble had set up a land attack in North Africa, and had suggested that the Bashaw's brother, who wanted the throne, should be encouraged in trying to get it. All this intrigue, plus the presence of those black-hulled ships off the harbor, were very discouraging to the Bashaw. Colonel Lear came over from Algiers and boarded the *Constitution* and soon white flags of truce were running between the frigate and the Tripolitan shore. In May came negotiations and a treaty, signed in the cabin of *Constitution*, where Preble and his boys had laid so many plans.

The Bashaw agreed to peace. There was to be no indemnity to anyone, and the American captives of the *Philadelphia* were surrendered on the final payment of $60,000.

The negotiations went on — and then the Bashaw attempted to drive a harder bargain, whereupon Commodore Rodgers turned cold. The treaty was signed on June 3, 1805, salutes were exchanged between the shore batteries and the ship that had battered them so often, and the Americans sailed away.

At about this time, the Bey of Tunis became troublesome. Over the last two years the Bey had tried to play both ends of the Tripolitan war, assuring the Americans of his adherence to the treaty between Tunis and the United States, but trying to send aid and trade into Tripoli at the same time. Half a dozen Tunisian ships had been captured by the Americans while trying to run the blockade. The Bey insisted that they be returned. The Americans insisted that they were booty and would not give them back.

In June the Bey threatened that he would begin taking American ships if they would not return his vessels. Commodore Rodgers heard of this threat, and in July moved the squadron over to Tunis to anchor. The frigates and the lesser ships sat there, not acting, but reminding the Bey and his officials that they had beaten Tripoli and they could do the same right here. For two weeks the Bey delayed serious negotiations, until Rodgers had the definite impression of unfair dealings and stalling. So Rodgers went into the cabin of *Constitution* and took up his pen.

The Bey had to do one of three things, he informed the American consul general in Tunis, and he had to do it without delay.

First, he must give the old guarantee of peace once again, or he must send a minister to the United States to negotiate, or he must negotiate the treaty over again right then and there. He could do it peaceably, or he could do it after the squadron attacked. For that would be Rodgers' next move.

The Bey negotiated, and the problem was solved. Never again would the Americans pay tribute to the Barbary pirates of any port.

*Constitution* stayed on to make sure the peace was kept. Commodore Rodgers went home in the spring of 1806, but the ship remained, the guardian of the American peace. Captain Hugh Campbell took her over, and kept her in the Mediterranean. By this time some of the men had been aboard for years, with virtually no shore leave, and the irritations and unfairness of it drove them to desperation. The Navy Department promised a relief, the *Chesapeake*. That ship was delayed — she got into a fracas with the British frigate *Leopard* off the Virginia coast, a disgraceful affair which nearly destroyed the career of James Barron, and which brought to a head American-British hostility.

From *Constitution*'s point of view, the affair kept the relief from coming, and the result was an attempted mutiny! It was suppressed and faded into the pages of maritime history. *Chesapeake* never did come; after the fight with *Leopard* she had to go into drydock at Norfolk, and finally *Constitution* came home without any relief at all. She went to New York and paid off her crew, and there was put up for a refit that lasted nearly two years.

The Barbary Wars were over. It was hard to remember that the pirates had ever been a problem.

# Chapter Three

## The Narrow Escape

In 1808, when *Constitution* had her refit in New York, the gunners of the Navy had some new ideas about the weight and type of guns that should be used aboard the frigates. They were thinking about the British, and there was no doubt about it.

*Constitution* had been built with extra heavy timbers, to accommodate heavy armament. But she was still a frigate, not a ship of the line, and the armorers sometimes seemed to forget that fact. She had her thirty long twenty-four-pounders down on the gundeck, but the refit added sixteen thirty-two-pounder carronades on the quarter deck, and on the forecastle two long bow chasers and six thirty-two-pounder carronades.

The carronade, to be sure, was not nearly so weighty a gun as the long gun. Those thirty-two-pounders had a bore of over six inches, but they were only four feet long, and altogether the metal was cast thinner than that of a long gun. The charge of powder to fire a carronade was only 2.5 pounds, compared to the six pounds to fire the long guns. The idea of the carronade was that of the battering ram, to be used at close quarters in a broadside against the enemy ship and knock her timbers to pieces.

But they were heavy enough, these new guns; they gave *Constitution* a total artillery of fifty-four pieces, and they changed her whole balance. She had been known as a sharp sailer before, but now she quickly won a reputation as a "wet ship before the wind" which meant she shipped quantities of water on the spar and gun decks, and she rode very heavily at her anchors.

Captain Rodgers did not keep *Constitution* long. He became disgusted with her sailing qualities, and when he was commodore of the Northern Squadron he wanted the fastest ship afloat. He transferred his flag, then, to *President* because she was believed to be a faster sailer. So then aboard *Constitution* came her old First Lieutenant Isaac Hull, one of the men who knew better than anyone else how she could be sailed under the proper conditions. They had done well for themselves, both these old acquaintances: *"Connie"* had a reputation that outdistanced her supposed sailing qualities. Hull, who had commanded the brig *Argus* during the war against the Tripoli pirates, had been commissioned captain in 1806. Another of Preble's boys had made a success.

Eighteen-ten was a dull year, as peacetime years were likely to be for fighting men and fighting ships. The Northern Squadron was assigned to New London, and made cruises to other ports. It might well have been disbanded, save for the *Chesapeake-Leopard* affair, and the growing feeling that war with Britain was coming near.

The spring of 1811 found *Constitution* at Annapolis, where she was sent to pick up the American minister to France, Joel Barlow, and take him and his family to Cherbourg. There was one delay after another; it was August before the ship sailed. She was five weeks to the French coast and when she arrived off Cherbourg, she found herself in the midst of a British squadron that was blockading the port. England and France were at war again.

The British were not pleased to see an American vessel in the area, and even less pleased to see a warship. The commander of the squadron sent a boat to *Constitution* and asked Isaac Hull to call on him. In reality, it was a sensible enough request, but under the circumstances of raw British-American relations, Hull refused to accept the invitation. The officer then asked that Hull delay his entrance into Cherbourg harbor until the next day. Hull refused.

For a moment it appeared that there might be war then and there, but the British backed away from confrontation with the prickly American captain, and he sailed in to deliver his passenger, and out once again on September 12, on a mission to deliver some gold to the Dutch.

A few days later Hull brought *Constitution* back to Cherbourg, to take an American diplomat across the channel to a new post.

That day, Isaac Hull very nearly did get into a war.

He sailed *Constitution* through the British line toward the port, and some of the British ships moved up with him, possibly to keep other ships from sailing out under cover of the American approach. Obviously it was a delicate situation, entering a war zone.

The French had previously given Captain Hull some secret recognition signals, but with the British tailing him he chose not to use them. And so the French batteries inshore began firing at *Constitution*.

One shot passed through the starboard waist nets, taking off the whole stern of the number two cutter, and through the mainsail. Another shot struck just aft of the forechains.

Then Isaac Hull remembered his signals.

A few days later *Constitution* crossed the channel. As she anchored and the passengers left, Hull and his officers realized how tense the situation between America and Britain was. It seemed that the British were determined to create an incident if they could do so. For here was an American warship, on a diplomatic mission, having just landed the new Minister to London, Mr. Russell. Under anything like normal conditions, the British warships at Portsmouth harbor would have outdone themselves in the courtesies; but now in these days, it was not so, and especially not with Americans.

Late on the evening of November 13, as the *Constitution* rode quietly at anchor, a boat came alongside, and the British lieutenant who came aboard identified himself as an officer from the British frigate *Havannah*. He asked for the captain, but Isaac Hull had gone to London with his distinguished passengers and Lieutenant Charles Morris was in command. The English officer was courteous; he informed Lieutenant Charles Morris that he had a deserter from *Constitution* who had swum to the English ship.

Next day, when Morris sent for the deserter, the British had changed their minds. He was told he could not have the man without the permission of the British admiral. So Morris went to the admiral, who raised the whole question of American return of British prisoners — but still did not get the man, Thomas Holland, because he was by then claiming to be a British citizen, and the admiral decided to retain him in the British ship.

A few days later Morris was disturbed at eight o'clock at night by the sounds of musketry, and when he went to the deck he discovered that an English seaman named John Burnes had swum over from the *Havannah*.

Morris was still fuming after the British treatment of the American flag in the Holland incident. Now he reciprocated — he sent a boat to announce to the *Havannah* that he had a British deserter aboard. When the British came the next day to collect him, Morris gave them the same story they had given him about Holland, and the British officer went off, furious.

The British were not used to reciprocal treatment, it seemed, for in the taverns and on the waterfront there was much talk about the "damned Yankees" and "getting their man, if by force."

A pair of British frigates moved in on the *Constitution* so close that it would be difficult to set sail and move out without fouling them and Morris knew that to foul them under these conditions would be to encourage an international incident.

Morris was saved from the need for a difficult decision by the return of Captain Hull, who quickly saw what was going on. When he heard the story of the deserters, Hull was as angry as any British admiral, and he decided he would play their game out. He ordered the *Constitution* moved down to St. Helen's Roads, and braved the frigates. The American seamanship was of very high quality these days — Hull was a spit and polish officer who demanded performance. And that was in the tradition of the *Constitution*, anyhow. During Preble's days in the Mediterranean, Lord Horatio Nelson had seen *Constitution* and the squadron under sail and had remarked on the precision with which the Americans moved their ships.

This day that precision paid off. Hull gave the orders, the sails were set, the anchor raised, and the *Constitution* moved out without touching either of the challenging ships, under her topsails.

While the ship moved, Hull let it be seen by the British that the gunners were busy, overhauling their guns and sending grape and round shot up to the shot lockers by every gun.

Within an hour of sailing, Hull saw behind him the pair of English frigates, which apparently had orders to shadow him and make life as difficult as possible. He anchored at St. Helen's Roads, and the frigates anchored there too, once again inhospitably close. There was no mistaking their unfriendly intent.

Hull pretended to pay no attention, but on November 21, when he was making ready for sea, his first action was unusual — to say the least — for a ship just leaving a friendly port. At half past three that afternoon the men at the capstan hove the anchors up taut, preparatory to raising them. The topmen got up sail, but as they did so the drummers beat To Quarters, the signal to prepare for action, and the gunners knocked open their ports and manned their guns. From the British frigates, the sight of *Constitution* readying for sea was the view of a ship preparing for battle.

Fifteen minutes later Hull ordered the ship under way, the capstan moved the anchor up, and the sails were clewed down and the yards shifted, and the *Constitution* began to move, threading her way between the British frigates, and heading for the clear channel.

One of the British frigates raised anchor and followed them to sea, but stood well back and observed the *Constitution*, which was ever ready for any action that might come.

This unfriendliness was a marked contrast to the treatment a few days later at Cherbourg, where Hull went once more to pick up dispatches from the American mission and take them home. Had he not fought the Undeclared War with France, Hull would not have recalled the days that were so different. Now he was entertained and complimented — he went up to Paris and there met General Lafayette and General Kosciusko, and many other Europeans who had helped the Americans in those worrisome days of revolution. It seemed a long, long time since those days, although only a quarter of a century had passed.

What with delays in Europe, a long passage home, and work around the capes, it was March before *Constitution* was home for leave, and laid up in the Washington Navy Yard for a refit.

Captain Hull took this opportunity to try to restore *Constitution* to her old fast-sailing pattern. He made a formal complaint about what had happened to her (not, however, blaming anyone) and suggested that she be docked and her bottom repaired. Perhaps the copper had loosened. There was only one way to do that job in Washington. She had to be careened, moved into shallow tidal water and then allowed to sit in the mud on one beam while the other was examined, then reversed at the next low tide. It was quite an undertaking, demanding the removal of all the heavy equipment of the ship and all the stores. Then the repairs took some five weeks.

*Constitution* was lucky here in Washington, for she had many friends among the staff. That was important, for a ship could get extra treatment or just the minimum. The Master of the Navy Yard, fortunately, was Nathaniel Haraden, who had been Preble's sailing master in the days of the Barbary Wars. Master Haraden *knew* how well she ought to sail, and he was totally sympathetic when Hull complained about his problems. So everything that could be done for *Constitution* was done. "Jumping Billy," as the Yard Commandant was known, had a few ideas of his own. He restowed the supplies to give her better flotation, which meant better sailing trim. He threw out about a third of the ballast put down by the Brooklyn Navy Yard earlier, and he assured Captain Hull that this would pull her back to that old twelve-knot speed she made so easily before. She could not have been in better hands.

The luck of it became apparent just a few weeks later, for war came to America with the declaration of the Congress that Britain's behavior had become intolerable. War was declared on June 18. Two days later, while Hull was ashore, the word came to *Constitution* and at five o'clock in the evening Lieutenant Read, the duty officer, turned out the crew on the main deck and read them the declaration. The crew shouted for a cheer, and the request was granted, so the men of *Constitution* broke into *huzzas* for the danger that would soon be threatening them. Their enthusiasm was real; the scandal of impressment and "sailors' rights" had touched home in every American warship over the past five years.

America was brave, but from a naval standpoint, most foolhardy. The United States government at that moment possessed only twenty ships ready for warfare on the sea, and three of these were half rotted out and should have been replaced. Congress suggested that the whole navy be brought into port and hidden from the British, and President James Madison seemed ready to accept that judgment until he was dissuaded by conversations with Captain Bainbridge and Captain Stewart. These officers indicated that it would be suicidal to let the British have access to American ports without a fight, and Madison was convinced.

The British offered a fearsome might at sea. They had then some seven hundred armed vessels. To be sure, a large number of these were in service on blockade of French ports, for the war with France still lingered. But the British Admiralty considered fifty vessels quite enough to seal off the Americas, and Whitehall was right — fifty ships could more than do the job against the slender resources of the United States. So the squadrons were sent out; line of battle ships with their sixty-four to a hundred guns; frigates, most of them rated as thirty-eights, which was the

British standard; and fighting sloops which might be shiprigged brigs or fore-and-aft rigged schooners. There was delay and confusion, for the British after all these years of war at sea were having trouble securing men to fight the ships. Half a dozen ships of the line and sixteen frigates assigned to the American station sat in British ports, while the press gangs hurried about the countryside, impressing farmers and even boys into service of the King.

With the outbreak of war, the American naval service received a shot in the arm. *Constitution* had often been manned by Irishmen and Swedes and even men of Naples, in the desperate shortage that Preble and his successors had felt. But the coming of war sent most merchant shipping scurrying for port, and until the owners saw how the wind would blow, they laid off their seamen. So more American sailors were available at the outbreak of the War of 1812 than had been ready to sail for the flag for twenty years.

Hull had his crew, had his ship ready for sea, and was eager for a fight. *Constitution* had never been better prepared than the day she first set out for the south after launch and her original fitting — or so it seemed.

On June 21, 1812, Hull had his orders. He was to proceed to New York and join the squadron of Commodore Rodgers once again. That was just three days after war was declared. Half his men were on leave and could not possibly be rounded up. Many of his officers had scattered across the country. But orders were orders, so Captain Hull told Lieutenant Morris to make ready for sea, with a half a crew, and Morris dolefully saluted and set about doing his job.

On June 25, she was at the mouth of the Potomac, the gunners still laboring to put the gundeck back in order after all the repairs. On June 28, she reached Annapolis, and here gained leave to find her crew and mount the stores she would need for a long voyage if necessary. In ten days all was put to rights, the crew was mostly aboard, and on July 5, she sailed down the Chesapeake, chased by brigs and sloops bringing supplies and the rest of the crewmen, and, on July 12, she passed out into the open sea, finally ready for what might come.

Each day at dawning the drums rolled and the men went to quarters, practicing warlike maneuvers until they were letter perfect. It had been more than half a dozen years since her guns were fired in earnest. At any moment they might encounter a British squadron or any number of British ships, all of which must be presumed to have adequate recent experience in the niceties of war. So the training was grim work, and the men kept at it until at nightfall they dropped exhausted into their hammocks.

One unnoticed fact of their situation was to become invaluable: the refit and the long period of *Constitution*'s crew ashore at rest.

As Captain Hull sailed down the Chesapeake

and made ready to find his way to New York, a whole British squadron was moving down on him. Sailing together were the ship of the line *Africa*, which mounted sixty-four guns, the thirty-eight-gun frigates *Shannon* and *Belvidera* and the thirty-two-gun frigate *Aeolus*. Separated from them, but a part of the unit, was the thirty-eight-gun frigate *Guerriere*, commanded by Captain James R. Dacres. He had been delayed and was north of the rest of the squadron.

At noon on July 17, *Constitution* was beating her way against the wind, heading northward in a series of tacks as she must. The wind was not only contrary, it was so light as to make the progress very slow.

Two hours later the lookout in the foretop of the *Constitution* shouted. Four sails had appeared on the horizon, heading down from the north, coming in toward the New Jersey coast.

The wind was from the northeast, which meant the other ships — if they were enemies — had "the weather gauge," or could sail down on *Constitution* and attack the American frigate while she was beating about to windward.

But were they enemy ships? They should be, according to all information, Commodore Rodgers and the American squadron that *Constitution* was scheduled to meet in these waters. Hull so presumed, and he headed *Constitution* up to meet them. He was too far off to see the triple tier of guns of *Africa*, which would have told him quite a different story.

Two more hours passed. Then came another shout from aloft — another sail, coming down from the north and heading to join the four.

It was slow going for *Constitution*, this beating upwind, and she seemed to make snail's progress toward the other ships. At six o'clock the wind failed altogether. The sea's gentle motion quit, and the water became so glassy the fading sun reflected as it would from a millpond. In the glare very little could be seen.

As darkness came, Captain Hull took the precaution of a good commander at sunset. He cleared the ship for action, the guns were run out, the men told to go to their posts and wait. Then, in the growing darkness, Hull ordered up the lights that were the signals among the American squadron members. The lights came up to the yards and burned and blinked there — but there was no answer.

Fifteen minutes went by. No answer.

Half an hour. Still no answer.

Hull was growing a little anxious. It was a clear enough night, and there was no reason he should not be seen by his fellows.

Three-quarters of an hour passed. No response from the squadron to the north.

It might be that some trick of the light kept the others from seeing him. It might even be that Commodore Rodgers had new orders of which he knew nothing. But to play safe, Captain Hull hauled down his signals, and turned his ship in the darkness and headed away from the others.

One ship followed.

At four o'clock in the morning the other ship was close enough on the southeast that its captain tried a recognition signal of his own: he fired one rocket and two guns. It made no sense to Captain Hull and the men of *Constitution*, and they suspected now the truth, that they were in range of enemy vessels. The ship in question so near them was indeed the *Guerriere*.

Hull was not going to reply to *that* signal, and he did not. Aboard the *Belvidera*, Captain Byron did see the *Guerriere*'s signal and recognized the ship for what she was. But he also had recognized that *Constitution* was an American frigate, and he was trying to entice Hull to come near. So he did nothing to help Captain Dacres. Dacres then came to the conclusion that all the ships were the Americans of Rodgers' squadron, and he turned down wind to escape what he saw was a superior force.

By this time Captain Hull saw that he was in the midst of his enemies, and must do something to escape or he would surely be captured or *Constitution* would be sunk.

The wind was so light they had drifted with flapping sails all night. At daylight Captain Hull could see one large frigate on her lee quarter. Two miles astern with all sails set came the ships of the British squadron — and that was easy to tell because now *all* the British ships ran up their colors.

They had wind, and Hull had none. They

gained on *Constitution*. Soon they came to within firing range and some of the frigates began to fire. Their shots passed over *Constitution* without doing any damage.

The situation looked completely hopeless to the junior officers and the crew. Lieutenant Morris' heart sank, and he was certain that he was destined for the bottom of the sea or a British prison ship within the span of the day. But Hull was not about to give up his ship without a fight. He set the gun crews to their work. A pair of twenty-one-pounders had been moved to the stern. The taffrail was cut away so they could fire directly aft. Two other guns were run out the cabin windows.

There were other measures to be taken. One was to slosh down the sails to close the fabric of the canvas. This way the ship could take maximum advantage of any breeze at all. And the men were put to work on the pumps — taking out twenty-three hundred gallons of fresh water to lighten her. If she survived this affair, there was plenty of fresh water ashore for *Constitution*, and if she did not she wouldn't need it any more. So out went the water to lighten her — even as the crews of the boats were ordered to begin to tow the ship.

For a time *Constitution* seemed to gain on her enemies, for they ran into the same lack of breeze and stopped, while Hull's measure bore fruit and the American ship moved away. But the British watched through their glasses, and followed suit.

They wet down their sails. They began to tow. Then, at eight o'clock in the morning, the British had a better idea. As the Americans watched through their glasses, they saw the crew of *Shannon* furling up her sails. All the boats available from the British squadron then concentrated on *Shannon*, towing cables were passed, and the full manpower of the squadron was exerted to catch up with *Constitution*.

This *was* a blow!

Lieutenant Morris was much disheartened. He could see the prison ship coming for him, as the *Shannon* gained steadily with her superior manpower.

Then a gust of wind caught the sails of *Constitution* and she forged ahead for a few minutes. The gust died, and she was still slightly better off than she had been fifteen minutes before.

But the men of *Shannon*'s tow team pulled inexorably, and regained the ground. Once more the future looked black.

Even though Lieutenant Morris was in despair, his brain continued to work. He recalled watching with awe one day when the captain of the *President* had taken her out of harbor by a strange means. *President* had been becalmed although there was a wind offshore, and her captain had put an anchor in a boat, had it rowed out to the end of the cable and dropped the anchor. Men on the ship had then turned the windlass, the anchor had caught in the bottom, and the frigate had begun to move, pulled by the power of kedging.

Morris suggested kedging here, and Captain Hull was quick to see that it might indeed work for them. Men were sent into the chains to sound. They found a bottom at twenty-five fathoms. So the launch and a cutter were lowered and sent ahead with a kedge anchor, to which was affixed a long line of hawsers and ropes. The bosun had scoured every locker and storage hideaway aboard the ship and put together a line nearly a mile long.

The ship was drawn to the anchor, every free man on deck pulling on the ropes and cables. When the anchor was at the ship's bow, it was picked up again and taken out, and the whole process begun again. Each time the wind failed the kedging began. As the wind quickened the kedging was stopped. And by this method the *Constitution* drew out of gunshot range of the British squadron. Only *Guerriere* kept up that forenoon, and harried the Americans by firing several broadsides, but the distance was too great and the shots fell short.

As the hours went on, and the British watched what the Americans were doing they were first puzzled, and then saw that the system was working. Captain Byron adopted the kedging plan — and improved upon it. He put together two anchors, one fast to each end of a cable passed through hawse holes forward. One anchor was sunk, and the men pulled the ropes. As the anchor rope came in, the second anchor was taken into a boat, and as the first anchor's distance lessened, the second anchor was carried out, until finally as the first anchor was drawn up out of the water the second anchor was dropped far ahead of the ship. There was no hesitation then aboard Byron's *Belvidera* — and she began to gain on *Constitution* once more.

All day long the grim race continued. *Constitution* showed her sailing grace, for each slip of wind was taken in and used as fully as ever a ship used the air. The men kedged and rowed, and pulled and hauled, and there was not an hour of sleep in bunk or hammock all day or all that night. Occasionally men were rested, falling down on the deck and napping for a few minutes, but the risk was too great — the danger there every moment — and the hauling must continue.

Watch on, watch off — the relief lay on the deck, and the gunners dozed atop their guns, waiting for the desperation of action against a whole squadron.

All night long the hauling continued, even when the cloud and darkness obscured the enemy vessels, for Captain Hull knew that the British would not stop, nor could he.

Morning came, and dawn found one British frigate out of range on the bow, two frigates on the beam, and one on the quarter, all to leeward. The *Africa* had given up the chase. She was far too heavy to be kedged or towed in that fashion and keep up. The smaller vessels of the squadron

97

were behind, on the lee quarter, taking advantage of the wind as they could. Four frigates ought to be able to deal with the single American ship, it would seem.

The ship on the lee bow was in the best position to attack *Constitution*. Captain Hull saw it as daylight brought the scene into focus. A few good tacks if the wind did not increase, and the enemy would be in position to begin firing.

On the port quarter stood another, smaller frigate, and if Hull could maneuver past this one, he might get away. It was worth doing and he tried. He headed for the ship, the *Aeolus*, and managed to pass her. For some reason she did not fire a shot at him.

So much, so good.

Now the danger came from the frigate *Shannon*. All morning on this second day, *Shannon* tacked and tacked, and she began to gain on *Constitution*, which had to sail that course to miss *Aeolus* and stay away from *Guerriere*.

But now, as if to answer American prayers, the wind freshened. Those who recalled *Constitution* of recent months were down in the mouth, for she was so bad a sailer on the wind — or had been since that New York refit. But Hull's memory went back further to the race for the cask of Madeira so many years ago, and as the sails caught and the hull strained beneath his feet, he sensed that Jumping Billy had done his job well at Washington Navy Yard. They piled on the canvas: topsails, topgallants, royals and studding sails and spanker and flying jib, as the wind kept increasing. At noon *Constitution* was making ten knots easily and by two o'clock in the afternoon she logged 12.5 knots and was pulling away from the enemy.

As the canvas caught and the sails were added, the boats were recovered, every one. Lieutenant Morris recovered his good cheer, and the men began to smile and walk about the decks with a new confidence.

At the rail, Captain Hull could smile too. Behind him he could see the British, cutting loose their boats or abandoning them so they could keep up the chase. That would give the squadron something to do for the next week — someone was going to have to recover boats and crews from this day's work.

Although drawing away, they were not out of it yet. And there was another danger, to another party. Up to windward came an American merchantman, flying the flag. Hull watched through the glass as the nearest English ship suddenly hoisted the Stars and Stripes. Such calumny! But it was typical — any ruse was acceptable in a chase; there was only dishonor if a ship fought under false colors, and not even always then.

But Hull was not going to stand by and watch an innocent American merchantman captured by the British if he could help it. Immediately he ordered the Union Jack run up the masthead, and seeing it, the merchantman cut away and was saved for another day.

Captain Hull now showed why he was known the seven seas around as one of the finest seamen in the American navy. Ahead as evening fell, he spotted a rain squall.

Immediately he acted.

He sent all hands to stations and the topmen aloft with very specific orders. Sails flying and full they approached the squall. The British behind looked on in awe — the crazy Americans were about to be dismasted.

But the men had their orders. They were at their posts in the rigging. The moment the wind struck with its renewed vigor, every bit of canvas was shortened. But by this time the ship was obscured in the squall itself, and the British chasers could not see what had happened to it.

Knowing squalls and the danger of dismasting, the British captains shortened sail and waited, expecting to come out the other side and see a mastless hulk awaiting their pleasure.

But Hull's men stayed in the rigging, and the moment the wind steadied and the rain stopped, they made sail once again. As the scattered and short-sailed British squadron came through the squall, the captains looked ahead. There was *Constitution*, drawing away, having added another mile on her, and her sails pulling merrily as she moved along.

One more night on deck, one more night the men and the officers slept at their posts. One more night of worry for Captain Hull. But as morning came, he looked aft through his glass, and all he could see were sails. The enemy was hull down on the horizon, and as he watched the sails, too, disappeared. Then it was time for the first rest in sixty hours. The watch was split, the relief was sent to hammock and to bunk, and for the Americans the crisis was over. One by one the British ships gave up, and turned back north-east to recover their boats, and finally to assemble in the wardroom of the commodore's flagship and explain to one another just how it was that the American frigate had gotten clean away.

# CHAPTER FOUR

## THE CONSTITUTION AND THE GUERRIERE

A very happy Captain Hull sailed now for Boston harbor, for he knew he could not run the blockade at New York. The British squadron was between him and Long Island. He would have to find some way to be in touch with Captain Rodgers or Washington and secure new orders.

So to Boston he went, and arrived in President Roads just outside the harbor, having been at sea for twenty-two days. Captain Hull went ashore and discovered all kinds of rumors had preceded him. The opposition party which hated the war had started the rumor that *Constitution* had sailed without any powder. He scotched that story soon enough. But when the report got out about his remarkable feat of seamanship in escaping the British squadron, a hundred Bostonians wanted to feast him. He demurred. Let them give credit to the men who deserved it, said Hull, to Lieutenant Morris and the other officers and the crew who had obeyed every order with alacrity at the time that it counted. Never had men worked harder to save themselves, and they deserved the accolades.

For five days Hull was lionized in Boston for it was a great relief to the people of that port to have a warship protecting them from a sally by the British. He sent word to New York and to Washington that he had arrived here, and then when the answer came from New York that no letters had been left for him nor any new orders given, he set sail on August 2.

Perhaps Isaac Hull suspected the truth: even as he put to sea a messenger was hurrying up from Washington, ordering him to remain in Boston port. The Navy Department had a strict protocol; Captain Bainbridge was senior to Hull and should have the *Constitution* since he was ready for employment. Hull would be given one of the smaller frigates instead.

But this change never came to pass because by the time the messenger arrived in Boston, Captain Hull in *Constitution* was out searching for the British and action.

It was the business of a naval officer to know the habits of foreign trading vessels. The British ships in North America customarily ran a triangle: Bermuda-New York-Halifax.

On the legs of the triangle, British shipping was most likely to be found, so Hull headed east from Boston harbor, up past the coast of Nova Scotia, and to the Gulf of St. Lawrence. On August 11 in that gulf he captured the British brig *Lady Warren*, took off the crew, and burned her. Next day he sighted another sail, chased, and took the British brig *Adeona*.

On August 15 *Constitution* passed Cape Race. At daylight as the cape came into view, so did five sails, and Captain Hull ordered Lieutenant Morris to begin the chase. The men had been standing at action stations a good part of every day, and few old tars would have recognized the "six week wonders," so proficient had they become at their duties in the yards and at the guns. Now that *Constitution*'s original sailing qualities had been recovered, she had little difficulty in overhauling the vessels, and as she came up Hull decided they were a fleet of four merchantmen, convoyed by a ship of war. The ship had a brig in tow.

*Constitution* overhauled them all rapidly. Aboard the ship there was a flurry of action, and the brig was cast off, just as she burst into flames and all the vessels scattered so the frigate might not capture them in a group.

Overhauling the first vessel, Captain Hull learned that she was a British ship that had been captured by an American privateer and had guaranteed to put in at an American port. But since that time, the ship had been recaptured by the British, and so she had a crew of Americans and British aboard her. It was very complicated.

The second vessel overhauled was the brig *Adeline*. She was an American vessel but then traveling under a British prize crew, for she had been captured by the enemy and was heading into the St. Lawrence to become a prize.

From members of the British prize crews, Captain Hull learned that the British squadron which had chased him so desperately was apparently cruising off the Grand Banks. He had no wish to run into four frigates and a ship of the line when all by himself, so he decided to head south, and see what he could find off New York, while he kept an eye out for Commodore Rodgers and the American squadron.

For two days Captain Hull cruised south, and again he went about his training. The four hundred and fifty men responded with a will. They had now seen action, and they were confident that they were fighting men. And so said Captain Hull too, he, who had not long ago written the Secretary of the Navy, "The crew are as yet unacquainted with a ship of war, as many have but lately joined and have never been on an armed ship before. . . ."

On August 17 another sail was sighted, and Captain Hull ordered the chase to begin. The other ship was a smart sailer, and the wind was favorable for her so she ran steadily, and it was hours before Hull could determine that she was a brig. More hours passed; *Constitution* gained but slowly, and it was the night of August 18 before Captain Hull began to come up. As he came, the men of *Constitution* saw the men of the other vessel throwing over heavy objects, in order to lighten ship and gain speed. But on that night of the eighteenth, *Constitution* came close enough to put a shot before her, and she stopped, as well she might in the face of those twenty-four-pounder long guns. Then a rueful Captain Hull learned that the chase had all been useless. The captive was the American privateer *Decatur*. She had carried fourteen guns, but a dozen of them had been jettisoned in the race.

One good bit of news came out of the encounter. Hull learned from the captain of the privateer that a British frigate sailing alone had been seen on the sixteenth, sailing southward, apparently cruising toward New York. Hull apologized for the inconvenience and sent the *Decatur* on her way, then he headed south again, once more toward the Gulf of St. Lawrence.

The breeze was light and from the west that night, so they sailed a reach. As the day grew older the breeze moved around to the northwest and increased, which gave *Constitution* her best, she was sailing with the wind on her starboard quarter, speeding along at nearly twelve knots, and making as pretty a picture as a ship could be.

Noon came and the dinner meal. The lookouts were quiet. Two bells struck, and then three — and then it was two o'clock in the afternoon, and the lookout on the foremast royal yard sang out.

"Sail ho!"

They called the captain then, and he came on deck with his glass while half the men climbed the rigging to see the stranger and try to identify her.

So far so good. She was a large ship of three masts, heading southwest. *Constitution* headed toward her, the wind gauge in Hull's favor, if it came to that.

An hour later the men of *Constitution* knew they had a frigate before them. Could she be American? They would have to find out.

Half an hour more passed. Then they knew, for the other frigate set her flag — the Union Jack — and made not the slightest effort to run away.

It was a thrilling moment for Captain Hull and the men of *Constitution*. They knew that they were standing on the brink of history, for this would be the first real encounter between an American and a British frigate. The *Chesapeake-Leopard* affair, in which the British *Leopard* had challenged and fired upon a half-gunned ship not really ready for sea, was no test or contest. Not until this day could the test be proved.

There was a test to be made. The frigate before *Constitution* was the *Guerriere*, that same vessel that had come so close by the ship in the recent long chase by the British squadron.

Captain Dacres of the *Guerriere* was so confident of the resources and fighting quality of his own ship that he had recently sent a challenge to Captain Rodgers of the squadron. He was willing — more, eager — to fight any frigate the Americans could put out before him.

Personally, Captain Dacres had a low opinion of *Constitution*.

"A bunch of pine boards."

"A fir-built ship with a little bit of striped bunting at her masthead."

These opinions were the common jokes of the wardrooms from Jamaica to Gibraltar. The British were so used to victory on the sea that they could not consider a situation in which the weak colonial Americans might defeat them.

And as for their own ship, Dacres' opinion was no greater than any other — the consensus of the British navy was that *Guerriere* was as fine a ship as his Majesty possessed.

As Hull ran down upon the *Guerriere*, the wind was at his starboard quarter. He could not ask for more, and he came quickly and gladly.

On the *Guerriere*, Captain Dacres consulted with the master of the American brig *Betsey*, Captain Orme, who had been captured earlier,

What was that vessel? he asked Orme.

The American captain looked through the glass and gave his opinion. She was most certainly an American frigate, he said.

Dacres at first doubted him. She came too boldly for what he knew of the Americans, he said.

Orme repeated his claim, and Dacres believed.

"The better he behaves, the more honor we shall gain by taking him," said Captain Dacres, not for a moment doubting the outcome.

And a little later he called the crew.

"There is a Yankee frigate; in forty-five minutes she is certainly ours. Take her in fifteen minutes and I promise you four months' pay."

It was at this moment twenty minutes past

four o'clock in the afternoon. Up went the battle flags and pennants, and out came the guns with snap and roll. At 5:05 Captain Dacres gave the order to fire, and the gunners discharged the starboard broadside. That meant 597 pounds of shot from sixteen eighteen-pounders on the gundeck plus eight thirty-two-pound carronades on the spar deck. In all, the British frigate carried forty-nine guns.

Of this first broadside not a shot hit — she was too far off. But Captain Dacres immediately turned about and fired his port broadside. Of this, most passed over the *Constitution*, but two shots struck home, without doing much damage.

Hull replied with shots from her bow guns.

*Guerriere* was twisting this way and that, to fire her broadsides, and to keep from being raked fore and aft by a broadside from *Constitution*. That was the worst danger in a fight of this sort, with the American frigate having the wind gauge. Minute after minute the two captains jockeyed for position, each trying to smash the other ship's sails and rigging, to injure the maneuvering capacity.

Up went *Constitution*'s ensigns and pennants at each masthead to show her defiance of the British enemy as Dacres had earlier shown his own. For three-quarters of an hour they fought this game of yawing and ducking, the British ship firing broadsides, and the American saving her shot, but using her long guns on the spar deck to reply.

This was slow warfare by Hull's standards, so before the hour was up he ordered the topgallant sails set, and headed directly for his enemy. Already the men of *Guerriere* had lost that four months' extra pay. And Captain Dacres now knew he was in a fight with a sailor who understood his trade.

*Guerriere* turned and put the wind on her port quarter, which meant the two ships were sailing the same direction, and their broadsides would soon open up on each other.

One shot from *Guerriere* came through the forward bulwarks, smashing wood into splinters that wounded the crew of one of the forward guns. The men wanted to fire, and Lieutenant Morris came to Hull with the request.

Hull said no. Wait.

When the men of *Guerriere* saw that they had "hulled" *Constitution*, they set up a cheer. The end of this Yankee enemy seemed near in sight.

Morris came again.

"The enemy has opened fire and killed two of our men," he reported. "Shall we return it?"

Captain Hull looked across the open water between the two ships. Not close enough yet.

"Not yet, sir," he replied.

Lieutenant Morris made the rounds again, and came to repeat his question.

Not yet, was the answer.

And a third time Morris came, and still the answer was to wait, even though the shot was coming heavy and the damage increasing.

Just then one shot struck the hull of *Constitution* square on, but instead of penetrating, it bounced and fell harmlessly into the sea.

"Hurray," shouted a seaman from the deck. "Look at that bounce. Her sides are made of iron."

And a cheer went up from the Americans for their gallant vessel.

*Old Ironsides* she would become, and old ironsides she was that day, as the smaller eighteen-pound shot of the *Guerriere* spanked against the extra heavy timbers that Joshua Humphreys had given *Old Ironsides*. That architect and builder had known what he was doing, the proof of it came right here this day in the broadside-to-broadside battle.

The *Guerriere* now steered away before the wind, and the stem of *Constitution* hung over the British frigate's quarter. Only a few yards separated the ships, and to Hull, this was the moment.

He stooped down, splitting his breeches from waistband to knee buckle in the effort, and then flung himself straight, shouting to Morris and his men.

"Now boys! Pour it into them."

The gunners had been waiting, matches lighted and with yell and cheer they obeyed their captain. The twenty-four-pounder balls, delivered at such close range, went crashing through the sides of *Guerriere*. Those fifteen twenty-four pounders and the carronades on one side delivered a broadside of 684 pounds of metal.

Nelson had urged his captains to close with the enemy — and here the American captain Hull was proving the point once again.

That first American broadside came at 6:05. For fifteen minutes the ships stood yardarm to yardarm, both crews firing with whatever they had at hand.

The British fired as they had been taught — fire, pull back, swab load, fire again — the gunners pulling the lanyards as soon as the gun was in position. But the Americans had been taught in a different school — they had a crude gun sight on those twenty-four pounders, and they had learned how to use it. Heavier shot and better aim began to tell. They were shooting for the spars and the rigging.

At 6:20 a shot from one of the guns struck the mizzen mast of the *Guerriere*, and down it went, over the starboard rail, to drag and make the British frigate hard to maneuver.

"Hurray, boys," shouted Captain Hull, snatching off his hat. "We've made a brig of her."

As he shouted, the real damage became apparent: *Guerriere* was dragged around by that floating mast until she was across the wind. Hull saw, and ordered the *Constitution* helm to port, as she forged on ahead of the other ship. The yards were swung around, the helm put hard aport, and as the starboard side of *Constitution* passed the bow of the *Guerriere*, the men of *Old Ironsides* fired a broadside that raked the enemy ship from stem to stern.

At that moment Captain Hull was remembering an old encounter with Captain Dacres in time of peace.

"If we ever meet in war," Dacres had said, boasting of his frigate, "I'll bet you a hat I take you."

There could be no more pleasant sight to Captain Hull's eyes than to see the main yard of *Guerriere* come tumbling down, as it did under that heavy fire.

Now the *Guerriere*'s bowsprit came near. *Old Ironsides* was not unhurt — many of her braces had been cut away and some of the sails were holed and of little use, so she was not responding as she did when totally uninjured. *Guerriere*'s bowsprit and jib-boom came poking over the deck of the American frigate, fouling the mizzen rigging.

The men at those spar deck guns of the *Guerriere* were shooting as well as they knew how, and one shot in the cabin of the American frigate started a fire, which called for some gunners to drop their weapons and move to save the ship.

They were putting out that fire, wondering if there would be boardings — for one man on *Constitution* was able to reach out of a cabin porthole and place his hand on the figurehead of *Guerriere*, right there before him.

Captain Dacres saw.

"Away, boarders," he shouted from the deck,

and tried to climb toward the bowsprit to reach *Constitution*'s quarterdeck. But Captain Hull had seen too, and his marines and fighting sailors were there, standing ready to repel and board themselves.

Lieutenant William S. Bush of the Marines hoped to lead this counterattack, and he jumped onto the rail — only to be shot dead by a British marine.

Lieutenant Morris, aft on the *Constitution*, saw that the fires were burning low, and he climbed the taffrail to see what was happening on board the enemy vessel. If he could only keep *Guerriere* entangled, how they could pour the shot into her!

Morris tried to pass a lashing around the *Guerriere*'s bowsprit to make sure it stayed entangled, but he was spotted by a sharpshooter from the British frigate, and shot through the body before he could accomplish his chosen mission. He fell to the deck, badly wounded.

At the same time, another bullet found Sailing Master John C. Aylwin, and he fell, wounded.

Those broadsides and the collision hurt *Guerriere* sorely, and it showed.

Captain Hull climbed up on the rail, but he was dragged back by a big seaman, who begged him not to lead the boarding until he had removed his captain's epaulets. He was too much the target.

As the captain was pulling back, a seaman fired a pistol at an enemy across the way, missed, and then in anger threw the pistol which knocked the British sailor down.

The Old Glory at the *Constitution*'s mizzen truck was shot down — and seaman John Hogan climbed back up and fastened it, with the balls of British riflemen whizzing about his head.

All this while, the *Guerriere* was taking severe punishment. Below deck, Captain William Orme, the master of the *Betsey*, was staying where he had been ordered by Captain Dacres, in the cockpit. He did not see, but felt "the tremendous explosion" of those raking broadsides, which made the *Guerriere* reel, and tremble as though they were passing into the shock of an earthquake.

He heard the mizzenmast fall. He saw the wounded men as they were dragged down to the cockpit for the ministration of the surgeon and his helpers. He stood there amid the moans and the shouting, and he waited.

The wind pulled *Constitution* clear, and she began to swing about into position to open fire again with those deadly broadsides. But as Captain Hull watched, the foremast and the mainmast of the British frigate toppled, and fell into the water, dragging all the rigging down, the sails caught and bellied and dragged the ship to a list so that the main deck guns were wetted.

She lay there, nearly alongside, rolling, an unmanageable wreck of a ship.

So much, it seemed, for Captain Dacres' boast. It had been two hours since the firing of that first gun from *Guerriere* opened the battle, and less than thirty minutes from the moment that Captain Hull split his breeches in his excitement of ordering the first *Old Ironsides* broadside.

Isaac Hull now ordered the helmsman to veer off from the shattered hulk that lay before them. The men turned to, out of gunshot to repair the rigging and clear away the debris of the well-fired British shot. The wounded were taken below for treatment, and the scuppers were cleared, the guns in shape to fight again. The gunners loaded and lit their matches again, and stood ready as *Constitution* wore back toward the floating bulk that had been the pride of the British frigate fleet.

*Guerriere* lay in the trough, the Atlantic swell rolling her main deck guns under with every cap of a wave. All the spars were down, and the sails dragged at her from the water. Some thirty round shot had penetrated her hull, to give it the appearance of Swiss cheese, four feet below the waterline. Her holds were full of water.

Of a crew of 272, the surgeon counted twenty-three dead or dying and fifty-six men wounded. On *Constitution* the casualties were small, seven dead and seven wounded. The ship hardly knew she had been in a fight.

Since there were no spars intact, no flag was flying aboard *Guerriere* when *Constitution* approached. Lieutenant George Campbell Read was sent off in a boat to approach *Guerriere*, hail

116

her, and discover the wishes of her captain. It was obvious that she could not run — but she still had guns and gunners and could still fight if that was what she wanted.

Was it?

Captain Dacres came to the rail. It was a hellish moment for so proud a man.

"I don't know that it would be prudent to continue the engagement any longer," he said in answer to the question.

"Do I understand you to say that you have struck?" asked Lieutenant Read.

"Not precisely," said Dacres, "but I don't know whether it will be worth while to fight any longer."

"If you cannot decide, I will return aboard my ship and we will resume the engagement," said Read, as ordered by his captain.

"Why, I am pretty much *hors de combat* already. I have hardly enough men left to work a single gun, and my ship is in sinking condition."

"I wish to know, sir," demanded Read, "whether I am to consider you a prisoner of war or an enemy. I have no time for further parley."

That was not quite true. Read had all the time in the world — Dacres had little time, for the ship might well sink beneath him soon. Dacres faced the dreadful moment.

"I believe there is no alternative," he said. "If I could fight longer I would, with pleasure, but I must surrender . . ."

"Then Commodore Hull offers his compliments," said Read, promoting his captain, "and wishes to know whether you need the assistance of a surgeon or surgeon's mate?"

He looked about. The bodies of the dead and dying were lying where they had fallen, some of them entangled in the mess that was the rigging an hour earlier. In some places adjacent port-holes and gun ports had been knocked into one great mess by the tearing of the timbers under the impact of those twenty-four-pound shot fired at close range.

Captain Dacres seemed undismayed. "Well, I suppose you had on board your own ship business enough for all your medical officers," he said.

"Oh, no," said Read, unable to resist the stab, "we had only seven wounded, and they were dressed half an hour ago."

Captain Dacres went then with Lieutenant Read to the *Constitution* to present his sword, as protocol demanded. Dacres had been wounded and it was difficult for him to climb the rope ladder to the deck of the American frigate, but he insisted on doing it himself, and went up hand-over-hand.

At the top stood a smiling, stocky Hull, to give this old acquaintance assistance.

"Dacres, give me your hand," he said. "I know you are hurt."

So up came the captain of His Majesty's late frigate *Guerriere*, that shattered mass that lay slopping in the water off the beam. A few words, one of the surgeon's mates took supplies and got into the boat, and was rowed off to the hulk to help with the wounded there. Dacres offered his sword, and it was refused.

"No," said Hull, "I will not take a sword from one who knows so well how to use it; but I'll trouble you for that hat . . ."

And so the battle came to an end. On the *Guerriere*, the scuppers were literally doused with blood. As the *Constitution*'s boat approached, the seamen could see their British counterparts throwing bodies overboard.

"The decks," said Captain Orme, "were covered with blood and had the appearance of a butcher's slaughter house; the gun tackles were not made fast and several of the guns got loose, and were surging to and fro from one side to the other."

The seamen had gotten into the grog, and many of them were drunk. The songs of the drunk, the sighs of the worried, the groans of the wounded melded into a bitter medley that told the story of the day's action. It was "a perfect Hell," said Captain Orme, before the Americans came in their boats, and took them all, wounded, uninjured, and the ten Americans who had been aboard as prisoners and impressed seamen. They were carried gently to the *Constitution* and they were cared for there, while Captain Hull took Captain Dacres into the cabin and made him as comfortable as possible.

Was there anything that Dacres wanted from

the ship? Hull asked. They had discussed the *Guerriere*, a row around her had shown how badly she was hurt, and that there was no chance of hauling her into Boston port, even as a trophy. She was no longer a ship, but a mass of timber and metal and rope and canvas, and she belonged for her own pride's sake on the bottom of the sea.

Yes, there was one thing Captain Dacres would like from the vessel if it still existed, and that was a family Bible, which was found and brought to the sad-eyed captain.

Then the process of transfer and dismantling continued.

At about two o'clock in the afternoon a sail was seen to the south, and all was interrupted as *Constitution*'s drums rolled and the calls were piped and she readied for action. But it was a false alarm, the sail went on about its business, and the work continued.

All night long the transfers continued. At daylight, Lieutenant Read reported that *Guerriere* had four feet of water in her hold and appeared to be in danger of sinking. They were very careful then, as they took the rest of the valuables from her.

In the afternoon of this second day all the work was done. A fire party went aboard the hulk and set it aflame. The yellow flickering grew higher, and the flames reached lower, until at 3:15 they reached the ship's magazine, and with a tremendous roar she blew up, sending a cascade of wreckage and flames and smoke high into the sky, before she sank, and left on top of the water only that flotsam that might have been expected.

*Guerriere* finished, Captain Hull set course for Boston port, even as the tall column of smoke from the last explosion stood over the wreckage on the water.

And on the way, in the wardroom and the gunroom where the midshipmen dwelt, and on the decks, the crews of the two ships talked among themselves and sometimes together about the glory of the action in which they had all fought so bravely.

Thus began the arguments that would continue for years. Some said that *Guerriere*'s timbers and her masts were rotten — and that is why she fell apart as she did under the battering of the *Constitution*.

That was a British claim.

Some said that the remarkable accuracy of the American gunners had done it. They had the gunsight, those big guns, and they aimed. When shooting in the beginning, they aimed for the rigging. Later, they waited until the *Guerriere* rolled and aimed for her copper plating, which put all those shots so deep below the water line.

Captain Dacres wondered at the irony of it all. He turned to Captain Orme, who until a few hours ago had been his captive. "How our situations have changed!" he said. "You are now free, and I am a prisoner."

There were some officers among the British who maintained their contempt for all things American. Of course *Constitution* would beat them, with those long twenty-fours to *Guerriere*'s eighteens. And as they walked the decks, they declared bitterly that *Constitution* was nothing less than a ship of the line in disguise. And that is what she really was, more or less — just as Joshua Humphreys had planned it.

# Chapter Five

## The Java

The voyage to Boston took a little more than a week, and when Captain Hull arrived, he anchored a mile and a half southeast of Boston Light. A few hours later he moved to Nantasket roads, a little way away, and prepared to move the British captain and the new captives ashore to facilities that were readying for them.

Then came quite a scare — on the morning after their arrival. A fleet of five ships appeared off the harbor, and Captain Hull slipped his cables and headed inside, sacrificing his anchors to avoid being caught in the roads by the British and cut off from the entrance to the harbor.

It was a sensible move, as any sailor would have agreed, but it turned out to be unnecessary. The squadron coming up was that of Commodore Rodgers.

What was done was done. *Constitution* moved into harbor at Long Wharf, to parole and transfer her prisoners and to make known to the port authorities her needs in supply and repairs.

The coming of *Constitution* was heralded in Boston from the moment she appeared off Boston Light dressed in bunting, the proud crew assembled, to announce the marvelous victory.

On the shore, lookouts saw and understood, and soon horsemen were galloping through the city and its environs, carrying the news of victory, although they did not yet know victory over what or whom. As the ship came in, cannon roared from the forts, and flags were unfurled.

When Hull's boat came ashore before he did, bearing the captain's official report, the sailors shouted out about the victory and the townspeople responded with glee.

And then the news spread like fire, people ran through the streets to talk about the *Guerriere* and *"Old Ironsides"* as she was called so affectionately by her crewmen. Crowds began marching in the streets, collecting fifes and drums, and singing patriotic songs. The mayor and the aldermen appointed a body of citizens to greet Captain Hull and his officers, and as she came into harbor they marched down to the port, as other citizens erected triumphal arches and the Ancient and Honorable Artillery Company, the oldest of military units, led the parade up through the streets. From the windows of the main thoroughfares ladies waved kerchiefs, and on the pavement the common people gathered with the businessmen and shouted themselves hoarse.

There was a reason for all the excitement. The hasty war was going badly for America. Detroit, out in the west, had been surrendered to the British by Isaac Hull's uncle, General William Hull. (It was ironic that the careers of the two

Hulls should meet with so much emphasis just then.) On the land the war was going slowly and a great many Massachusetts men, who had not favored the war in the beginning, were losing heart for it entirely. So Captain Hull's arrival with the wonderful news of victory was greeted with more enthusiasm than one could hardly imagine.

There was a scare for a day or so about the British squadron, and the celebration was held up, while Commodore Rodgers ordered the *President* outside port to look for the British, but that turned out to be a false alarm, and on September 5, the celebration was brought to a climax by a formal dinner in honor of Captain Hull and his officers. In the months earlier Boston had been wracked with political differences over war and trade with Britain. These differences were put aside this night, and all the leading citizens joined to pay homage to the national heroes.

There were speeches and prayers and poems in honor of the ship and its crew. In Washington, the Senate and the House of Representatives called special attention to the glorious deed. All this while Hull and his men were marching up State Street, and stopping at Faneuil Hall for the victory dinner, where seventeen separate toasts were drunk in honor of the Nation, the Navy, the Victory, and the Captain and His Officers.

The Congressmen, timing their celebration for the same hour, cheered as the report of the victory was read, and voted a special gold medal to Hull, and $50,000 in lieu of prize money for the officers and crew of *Old Ironsides.*

And then Captain Hull and Lieutenant Morris went off on a whirlwind tour of other major cities, to celebrate the victory and raise American morale for the struggle with Britain. They went to New York where they were met by Mayor DeWitt Clinton and given the key to the city. Merchants donated money for handsome swords for the pair and all the other officers, in honor of the victory. Hull sat for his portrait which was later hung in City Hall.

In Philadelphia, they received silver plate and other presents, and so did the rest of the officers of the ship who had served in this battle.

Meanwhile, *Constitution* was readying for sea again, almost as soon as Captain Hull and his officers left the ship's decks. Captain William Bainbridge came aboard and took command on September 15. He would be commodore of a new squadron, and she would be his flagship. The crew did not much like the change, and they threatened mutiny. Indeed, several dozen men were discharged in Boston then for outrageous statements and behavior. Some did not like Bainbridge. More simply wanted to continue under Hull.

The squadron was to include the frigate *Essex* under Captain David Porter, and the sloop of war *Hornet,* under Lieutenant James Lawrence. *Essex* was at Philadelphia, so on October 27, when Bainbridge sailed, he had only *Constitution* and *Hornet* with him. *Constitution* stopped at the island of Ferdinand de Nornonha for water and to leave a message for *Essex*.

Bainbridge's task was most delicate. Fernando de Nornonha was a Portuguese possession, a penal colony, in fact, populated by a handful of miserable prisoners and their guards and a colony of hogs and goats and chickens for the rest.

Bainbridge had made elaborate precautions to give information to Porter, yet not tip his hand to the inquiring British if they appeared. He left a letter addressed to Sir James Yeo, discussing old times in England, and signing himself as Captain Kerr of His Majesty's ship *Acasta*. But there was also a secret message on the paper, written in sympathetic ink.

"I am bound off St. Salvador the thirteenth of December; the *Hornet* was sent into the harbor with the subjoined letter. . . ."

Unfortunately the *Essex* never caught up with Bainbridge, but missed him at several cross-points, and then went into the high seas for adventures of her own.

*Constitution* was off for a new adventure, bearing the hopes of Americans, who had taken heart in their new navy with the adventure of Isaac Hull against *Guerriere*, as one poet wrote:

Ye tars of Columbia, whose glory imparts
New charms to the blessings your valor secures,

Oh! High be your hopes and undaunted your
 hearts,
For the wishes and prayers of a nation are
 yours.

Bainbridge's assigned task was to intercept
British merchant ships and destroy them. The
idea was to create so much confusion and un-
happiness in the British West Indies that in
London the king would recognize the rights of
Americans and settle for a peace that the government in Washington would find honorable. As
far as navy men were concerned the War of 1812
was not a war for territory at all, but to stop the
discourtesies and hardships the British imposed
on American shipping by their practice of impressing sailors or claiming "deserters" from
various American vessels.

In furtherance of the task, Bainbridge now
took *Constitution* and *Hornet* to San Salvador,
where he arrived off the port on December 13.

Captain Bainbridge was having his troubles.
The enlisted men of *Constitution* had been very
unhappy to lose Captain Isaac Hull, so angry as
virtually to mutiny. Only Hull had been able to
persuade them that it was all for the best. On the
voyage south the men were restive. Bainbridge
was a disciplinarian, taking stern measures to accomplish what Hull had apparently done with a
glance and a smile. Men were flogged, the pre-
scribed dozen lashes and no more. Men and boys
were sent aloft for punishment or even into the

brig. They were deprived of rations and rights. The punishments were heavy and frequent — although, of course, nothing like those vicious floggings aboard the British ships of war — and the crew and the officers drew away from one another. It would take something as heroic as another *Guerriere* action to bring them together again.

When the two ships arrived off San Salvador (Bahia), Bainbridge sent Captain Lawrence and *Hornet* into port with a letter to U.S. Consul Henry Hill. Bainbridge was a good commander, no matter his way with the men, and he asked a number of questions about the facilities and attitudes of the Portuguese who controlled Brazil, since he planned to be working those waters. He also wanted to know all the consul could tell him about the British, the number of ships of war in the area, their ports of rendezvous — everything, in fact, that an American war commander could wish to know about the enemy and supplies in a huge area of the oceanic world.

When Lawrence sailed in with his questions, he found a British sloop of war inside. She was the *Bonne Citoyenne*, under Captain P. B. Green. One of Lawrence's first actions was to issue a challenge to the British captain to come outside and fight. The frigate *Constitution* would not engage in the fight, he said. It would be between *Hornet* and *Bonne Citoyenne*.

There was a difference between American and British attitudes in this war: the Americans were inclined to be romantic and the British very practical. If *Bonne Citoyenne* won such a battle, Captain Green was quite sure the frigate would then come up and blow him out of the sea with her superior guns. So Green refused the challenge. It was all done very gallantly, through consuls as intermediaries. But the result was nothing, except that a furious Bainbridge and a furious Lawrence met and decided that Lawrence would remain outside San Salvador and wait for Captain Green to come out, while *Constitution* went off to seek other enemies of America.

Bainbridge sailed on December 26, leaving behind him a tangle of diplomatic quarreling, for the governor of the area took violent exception to the virtual blockade of his port by the Americans after *Bonne Citoyenne* would not come out to fight. Before raising anchor, Bainbridge made arrangements to meet Lawrence at sea, and then moved out.

Three days later as the sun came up *Constitution* was cruising along the coast of Brazil, about thirty miles southeast of San Salvador in a gentle breeze, moving under short sail, really loafing along. It was promising to be a beautiful day, with the wind blowing from the northeast, flecking the long swell with whitecaps.

The men were up. The "housekeeping" had been done for the morning, the ship flushed and scrubbed down, the guns cleared and inspected, the men fed and at their posts, lounging as sailors will on a good day with no sail in sight. Suddenly at nine o'clock the lookouts sang out that a sail — no, two sails — had been sighted on the weather bow, and within the hour, before they could be recognized very well, one of the sails set a new course, and stood off shore to head toward *Constitution*.

It was plain that the ship coming was a man of war, looking for a fight.

Bainbridge sailed on while he watched carefully. At 10:45, he tacked north and west, to get a look at her beam — it was hard to tell what kind of vessel she was from the head-on approach. The other ship was coming down the wind, which gave her an advantage, just as *Constitution* had had that advantage in the fight against *Guerriere*.

He came about again, to draw her offshore, and to gain searoom for a fight — because now Commodore Bainbridge was relatively certain he faced a British ship of war. The mainsail was hauled and the royals were taken in, for he had no desire to run from the other vessel.

Before the hour ended, the other ship ran up a string of signal flags that made no sense at all to Bainbridge. At 11:30 *Constitution* responded with her own recognition signals — and they were obviously as confusing to the other captain. So now Commodore Bainbridge was quite sure he faced an enemy, and he increased his preparations for battle.

His first care, because of all the difficulty with

the governor of San Salvador, was to draw the other ship well off the neutral coast, and so he put on sail and eased out his sheets, and the two ships ran on parallel courses out to sea. Bainbridge was now fairly certain that he faced an English frigate. He did, indeed, she was the *Java*, one of the fastest and best sailers in His Majesty's navy, under Captain Henry Lambert, an experienced and brave officer of the Royal Navy.

Lambert had the advantage with the weather gauge, and he was careful not to lose it, staying upwind of *Constitution* all during this race out to sea, gradually overhauling *Constitution* and making his guns ready for the coming fight.

Just after noon the captain prepared even further. *Java* ran up her British ensign to the mizzen peak, with a Union Jack at the mizzen topgallant masthead and another lashed to the main rigging. There was no doubt; she was British to the core.

Bainbridge ordered his own flags up, Old Glory at the mizzen peak and the main topgallant masthead with a Union Jack at the foremast to show that he recognized his enemy.

It was now quarter past noon. The weather continued fine, with spanking breeze blowing steadily.

The men of *Constitution* had their dinner, and a smoke, and prepared for the fight ahead. The commodore's own pennant ran up the mast.

Just before 1:30 Commodore Bainbridge was

satisfied that he was far enough offshore that no maneuvering would trouble him, and so took in the mainsail and royals, tacked the ship, and stood toward the *Java*, challenging, ready for battle.

Twenty minutes later *Java* turned, ready to deliver a raking broadside that was designed to smash *Constitution*, bow to stern. They were well inside long range.

Bainbridge saw, and ordered the ship worn away, presenting once more her flank to the enemy — if it was to be broadsides, it would be ship to ship.

At two o'clock sharp, Commodore Bainbridge was steering south, as close on the port tack as *Constitution* could sail, and this was remarkably well. *Java* was on the same course, to windward, still keeping the weather advantage.

And both were to start fighting. Captain Lambert hauled down his colors, save the Union Jack at the masthead. Could she be a merchantman only?

Nonsense, said Bainbridge, and ordered a long gun fired across her bow. The puff and the slamming noise of the shot and a broadside sent those navy colors flying back up, and an angry Captain Lambert fired a whole broadside, which was well-aimed and smashed into *Constitution*, while *Old Ironsides'* first volley fell short.

Now the firing became general. The tactic of Captain Lambert was to close so that his eighteen-pounders and his carronades on the spar deck might be useful. Commodore Bainbridge knew that with the enemy having the weather gauge his advantage lay in wearing away to maximum range of the twenty-fours, which kept the eighteen-pounders off, and still enabled him to hit the enemy.

It was tenuous work, running, and then hauling and tacking and trying to keep distance and keep from being raked by the enemy vessel, and Commodore Bainbridge paced his quarter deck as he watched the progress of the enemy and gave directions to his fighting divisions.

As the firing increased in tempo, a haze of smoke began to rise between the ships, and blow gently with the wind above them.

The gunners of *Constitution* had their orders — aim for the enemy's spars and rigging and cut them down if they could. The sailing crew had orders, keep as far away from those eighteen-pounders as possible, while keeping *Old Ironsides'* guns in range. The Marines had their orders — watch for the officers in their distinctive hats and coats, and shoot them down if possible.

The orders were nearly the same on board the *Java* — except she was trying to close every minute. Captain Lambert told his first lieutenant, Henry D. Chads, to bring those eighteen-pounders into play, to maneuver and try to rake the elusive American frigate.

At 2:10, *Constitution* was firing grape and canister shots aimed at cutting the sails and tearing the hempen rigging to pieces. They were well off the *Java*, even further than Bainbridge wished to be for accuracy. He moved in closer.

As he did so, one of the British marines fired and found his mark. A musket ball struck Commodore Bainbridge in the thigh, and sent him tumbling against the wheel of the ship, where he leaned to stay on his feet. Men rushed to him but he waved them away. The ball had missed bone and artery, and gone through. The wound was painful but not immediately dangerous.

Fifteen minutes later the Commodore had another narrow escape, as the guns of *Java* found their mark more and more often. The wheel of *Constitution* was shot completely away from under the Commodore and he had to move his position, while the steering moved two decks below.

Captain Lambert's tactic seemed to be to stay out of range of *Constitution*'s guns, except to run in and fire, while waiting the chance to rake the American ship. It was a sensible tactic for the faster British ship — like a boxer who darts in and smashes his opponent and then darts away again before the slower, bigger man can move.

But in this case the fight did not go along Marquis of Queensbury theory. Ten minutes after the wheel was shot away, Commodore Bainbridge ordered the frigate to close with the enemy, even at the expense of raking. *Constitution* set her foresail and mainsail and luffed up close to the *Java*, which ran free, and forged ahead. The ships were soon within musket range again.

This seemed to be just what Captain Lambert and the *Java* wanted. *Java* reached forward until she was off *Constitution*'s port bow, and the angle was too great for all but the bow chaser guns. She squared away to cross the bows of *Constitution* and deliver that deadly raking fire which might decide the course of the action in the next moment or two.

But Bainbridge knew. He shouted orders, and just as the prime moment came, off went *Constitution*, turning to parallel the British frigate and avoid the shot.

The ships headed west, even as the American sailors congratulated themselves. Three times now they had avoided raking by the skin of *Constitution*'s bow and the art of her Commodore's seamanship. For Bainbridge took advantage of every bit of natural cover — each time *Java* headed across to rake, he moved, fired a broadside, and then moved again under cover of the smoke so that the faster vessel must start this stalk all over again.

At 2:50 on one of these close maneuvers, the *Java* came up so close on a tight turn that her jib boom fouled in *Old Ironsides*' mizzen rigging. It appeared certain that the men of *Java* were trying to board the American frigate. Bainbridge saw, and ordered his fighting men aft to repel boarders.

The officer who led the Americans speeding aft was Lieutenant John C. Aylwin, already a hero of the action against the *Guerriere*, and one wounded in that fight.

Aylwin drew his pistol and jumped up on the *Constitution*'s quarterdeck hammock netting to fire. He aimed at the crowd of sailors and marines on the *Java*'s forecastle, just as the jib boom struck, and the ships shuddered in the impact of the crash.

On the *Java* a marine saw, and raised his musket. He fired. The shot hit Aylwin in the same shoulder that had been wounded aboard *Guerriere*, and he fell back to the deck. Just then a marine in the mizzen top of *Constitution* spotted an officer's blue coat on the quarter deck of *Java*, and he fired. Captain Lambert fell, shot through the left breast, just as the two ships clashed, and then drifted apart.

Men rushed up to carry Aylwin below, but like his Commodore, he refused to leave the fight and continued at his post.

Aboard *Java* Captain Lambert was out of the fight very badly wounded. Lieutenant Chads took over and brought the ships closer together. The British knew that to stand off and fight the *Constitution*'s battle was to risk the loss of their own ship without being able to do sufficient damage to the more powerful, stouter vessel.

Around they came again, the American topmen pouring fire into the decks of *Java*, each ship raking the other at the slightest opportunity, the *Constitution* firing round shot, grape, and canister and doing frightful damage.

Commodore Bainbridge was hit again — another painful, but not too serious wound. He was offered aid to go below, but he grimaced and refused. He was in this fight to stay.

Five minutes after the ships were fouled, *Constitution* was trying to rake; *Java* was trying to close and board. *Java* headed down on the American frigate, even though it meant another raking, and the sails of *Constitution* were backed to hold her where she was so that deadly fire along the length of the British ship could be continued as long as possible.

A minute or two of the tremendous impact of long guns and carronades must have their effect. *Java*'s bowsprit and jib boom fell, shot away by the round shot and ripped loose by the grape and canister from the carronades.

It was three o'clock. The battle had been in progress for fifty minutes.

Lieutenant Aylwin was still on deck, struggling to retain consciousness, but not willing to go below.

Aboard the *Java*, Captain Lambert was laid carefully down and supported. The decks were literally running with blood, and wounded and dying were all about him, victims of those dreadful rakings by the American ship. Midshipman Edward Keele was struck and wounded dreadfully — a boy about thirteen years old aboard his very first ship. As the fighting continued, the *Java*'s surgeon had him brought down to the cockpit, and with the sound of cannon roaring amputated the boy's leg.

Bainbridge, a shot through his thigh and a copper bolt driven deep into his leg, managed to support himself aboard the *Constitution*, directing the fire and the movements of his vessel, as he sought to stand off and rake, and Lieutenant Chads tried to close and board before the British frigate was dismasted.

Bandaged, ragged, and hardly able to support himself, Bainbridge stood there, a lean hawk, and he gained a new respect from the men of *Old Ironsides*.

It was after three o'clock in the afternoon, and the sun was beginning to lower, as if anyone aboard the fighting ships had a moment to consider so unimportant a matter. *Java* headed down again across *Constitution*'s bows, and Bainbridge turned. Another raking and *Java*'s foremast began to tumble, pierced by a twenty-four-pounder round shot, and to fall by the boards. Chopped off, the rigging snapping, it dropped over the lee bow.

It was five minutes past three o'clock. The sun had hardly lowered another degree.

The hail of accurate fire from the American guns continued. At ten minutes past three *Constitution* reached off *Java*'s bow, and then wore around to bring the opposite broadside into play. The broadside ripped out, again Bainbridge turned, and brought the first broadside back at aim and it fired. Port broadside, starboard broadside — all the while *Java* was staggering, mushing along under the weight of that dragging foremast.

Three fifteen: another broadside and *Java*'s main topmast came tumbling and crashing down from on high, the gaff and boom and spanker following.

More terrible broadsides, holing the hull at the water line the way the *Constitution*'s gunners had been taught to do, watching and waiting for that show of copper on the surge and ebb of the swell, aiming for the rigging, the marines in the tops watching constantly for officers or men engaged in vital tasks so they might pot at them with muskets.

Three fifty-five: another broadside (among many) and *Java*'s mizzenmast fell, carrying down the Union Jack, so that for the first time in the battle, the British frigate bore no colors at all. She was a wreck, mastless, steerage lost, sitting there helpless except for her guns and her own marines, who crouched now on the decks firing at the American gunners and any men they could see moving behind the rail of *Old Ironsides*.

During all this battle *Old Ironsides* had lived up to her name, for she was not badly hurt. The bulk of the damage to the hull had been accomplished by that first broadside or two of the *Java*. As for the rest, the gunners of the lighter ship had cut up *Constitution*'s rigging somewhat. If she were to engage in further fighting, it would be well to make some repairs.

The dismasting of *Java* naturally gave Commodore Bainbridge the feeling that the battle was over, even though the British ship continued to fire as he ordered *Constitution* worn away from the other ship while the repairs were made. Often it took a bit of time for a captain to get orders below decks, particularly in the heat of battle.

So *Old Ironsides* moved off, the Americans cheering loudly as that last mast dropped into the water. John Cheever, an American seaman, who was lying apparently dead on the deck opened his eyes and, calling out, asked what the noise was for. He was told, and he raised himself, cheered, and then fell back, dead.

Aboard the *Java* young Midshipman Keele sensed the cessation of fire from the protected spot where he had been laid, after his leg was taken off. What was happening? he asked anxiously. Had the ship struck her colors?

They could tell him no quite honestly, for Lieutenant Chads was trying desperately to raise the Union Jack on a jury mast.

Young Keele saw that a flag had been spread over him as a cover. What flag was this, he asked. It was the English flag, the flag of St. George, the flag of the King, and his flag he was assured. And the boy smiled, then, and died.

It was sixty-five minutes from the beginning of the action, and Bainbridge was confident that it was all ended. As he looked back at his enemy, she was floating like a hulk, no mast in sight, her colors down. But as he watched, Chads succeeded in raising the Union Jack aloft once more on his jury mast.

So now what?

Bainbridge shot on ahead of the other vessel, and his men climbed aloft with knife and line to reeve and repair. *Constitution* had taken a shot through the mizzenmast, and some of her other spars had been clipped by round shot or grape. Some more had been grazed and needed looking to. Her running rigging had taken a beating, and her shrouds and stays had been slashed. But that was all, save the damage on the deck and the killing and wounding of men. She was fit for another fight against an untouched enemy, so luckily and skillfully had she been brought through this performance.

As Bainbridge waited, painfully supporting himself until this action might come to an end, in spite of his pair of wounds, the first lieutenant swiftly got the casualty report from the ship's lieutenants. Eight seamen and one marine had been killed. Lieutenant Aylwin and two seamen were sorely hurt and not expected to survive. Twelve of her seamen were hurt seriously, and seven seamen and two marines were slightly hurt. For such an engagement the casualty list was nearly nothing; Bainbridge could be proud.

When the damage was repaired to his satisfaction, Bainbridge cast a speculative eye at *Java*. There was that Union Jack — which meant she was ready to fight. But never in his experience had a ship been less a ship than this.

Still, the rules and responsibilities were fixed: unless the captain of that other vessel hauled down his flag, they were still fighting over there.

If Bainbridge were to move away, the ship might be repaired and escape. If he were to send a boat, the other would have every right to blow that boat and all the men out of the water.

So if the Englishman wanted to continue the battle, then *Old Ironsides* would carry it to him.

At 4:20 Bainbridge moved his ship toward the enemy and an hour later was in position athwart the bows. One of those deadly broadsides turned directly on the ship, ready to rake that entire deck with fifteen twenty-four-pounders on the gundeck, and all those carronades fore and aft.

Lieutenant Chads knew then how hopeless it must be. Most of his guns were knocked out by the accurate fire of those *Constitution* gunners in the earlier phase of the battle. His captain was dying. Men lay on the decks, the dead and wounded almost inseparable, some of them pinned under the wreckage from the rigging.

True, Chads had worked valiantly, clearing wreckage, getting that spare spar tied to the stump of the foremast and another to the bowsprit so that he had a way of keeping up canvas. All this time he had worked and worked. Now he thought.

And as the lieutenant thought, he could envision the carnage that would come to his ship now if the virtually unhurt bigger vessel turned those broadsides on to rake her even just once or twice.

At half past five, Lieutenant Chads had the Union Jack run down. He surrendered.

Bainbridge was relieved. No victorious captain of the sea liked to slaughter enemies who were helpless. He thought Chads' action prudent, and was grateful that he did not have to bring more loss of life to the engagement.

There had been plenty. Although the exact figure of the casualties of *Java* was long argued, Bainbridge's account made it at sixty dead and one hundred seventy wounded. No matter the figure, the number of casualties was very great, as it must have been in so unequal a fight, with the bigger ship dismasting and blasting the decks and hull of the smaller.

With the surrender, the *Constitution* sent its boats to the side of the stricken vessel, and began moving the wounded off, while the British buried some of their dead at sea. One of the last of the wounded to come away from the hulk was Captain Lambert, who was unconscious at the time. His sword was delivered to the Americans by his officers.

After Lambert had been brought aboard, he was delirious for a time, but then he recovered consciousness, and Commodore Bainbridge was informed that his enemy was lucid. Bainbridge was resting, his wounds troubling him painfully, but he arose, with the aid of two of his officers. He could no longer walk alone. Supported by them, Bainbridge hobbled down to Lambert's cot, and there placed the enemy's sword in his hand, and spoke for a few minutes of the gallantry of the English in the action.

The sorting out of the people of *Java* was a

hard task. One of those to come aboard was General Hislop, the newly appointed Lieutenant Governor of Bombay in India, who was on his way in the *Java* to his new post when the English frigate was accosted this day.

Bainbridge had quite a start when the boat came to his ship to deliver this British officer. A few nights before the battle, Bainbridge had dreamed of fighting an English frigate, which he captured after a long battle. And for some reason, quite incomprehensible in the dream, there was a general aboard the naval vessel, a general who surrendered to him.

When Hislop's boat came off the *Java* and approached the *Constitution*, Bainbridge turned paler than he ought, even with his painful wounds. He turned to one of his lieutenants and spoke.

"That is the man I saw in my dream!" he exclaimed.

# CHAPTER SIX

## CAPTAIN STEWART'S ADVENTURES

When the long twenty-four-pounders of *Constitution* worked over an enemy frigate, they destroyed it. The case of *Java* was the second, for although it would have been preferable to keep the hulk and rebuild her as a part of the young American navy, Bainbridge and his officers decided she was not strong enough to make the voyage, for it would take sixty days to reach New York, and he did not believe she would hold out.

He might have taken her into a Brazilian port, such as San Salvador, but after his encounters with the governor's decided haughtiness, Bainbridge feared that the Portuguese might manage to deliver *Java* back into the hands of his enemies. Rather than that, he decided to fire the ship, and on the afternoon of December 31, she was set afire, all useful provisions having been removed from her. At three o'clock her magazines went up with a tremendous roar, and soon all that was left of the once magnificent frigate was a handful of flotsam.

There was one other souvenir — her wheel was removed before she was fired, and fitted to the *Constitution*, to take the place of the one shot out from under Commodore Bainbridge in the fight.

So it was back to San Salvador early in January, and on the second day of that month, Commodore Bainbridge landed his prisoners under parole that they would not fight again. Captain Lambert, pale and suffering, would die soon enough from his wounds. The general and his staff went ashore, as did some three hundred British naval officers and men, and when they were landed, the general presented to Commodore Bainbridge a gold-mounted sword in gratitude for the kindness with which the American had treated their enemies after the battle was ended.

Then it was back to Boston, to seek new orders and announce the victory. Bainbridge needed rest and recuperation. It was time for someone else to take *Old Ironsides* out to sea.

They sailed from San Salvador on January 6, leaving Lawrence in *Hornet*, still playing cat and mouse with *Bonne Citoyenne*, to the fury of the Portuguese governor.

Lawrence was to have many adventures of his own — to be chased by a British ship of the line here and later to capture a British brig before he reached port. But the squadron, as such, was effectively broken up with Bainbridge's sailing for America; *Essex* never did report, but was engaged in glorious battle off South America.

So the ailing Bainbridge turned to Boston, and on February 28, he arrived there, to land next day and be celebrated as Hull had been fêted before him. There were parades and dinners, and presentations. Congress voted him thanks and a medal, and even the state of Massachusetts, which was notably opposed to the whole war effort (because it hurt business) unbent enough to congratulate this hero of the sea.

When Bainbridge arrived, he learned that the $50,000 voted for the men of *Constitution* after the victory over *Guerriere* had not been paid to anyone's account. Another $50,000 was voted for the men on the capture of *Java*. Bainbridge complained and used his new vigorous influence — the money was paid, and then there were celebrations indeed in Boston town.

But while the Americans celebrated, the British lamented, and accused the United States Navy of the vilest of practices. In the last few months, Britain had lost three of her finest frigates, all in individual battle with American frigates. Following courts of inquiry and examination, the British were learning an unwilling respect for the American service, but they were also furious because Americans called their ships *"frigates."* It was the heavy hull and the twenty-four-pound long guns that made the difference.

In fact, the British Admiralty was not giving America the same credit given by the officers and men who had fought the Yankees in these battles. For when he was defeated and hauled down the Union Jack that December day, Lieutenant Chads remarked (and he repeated the remark later) that the Americans had sailed and fought their ship with exceeding skill, so much that he wished they were Britons.

No, it was not just the guns and the heavy oak that made *Constitution* what she was — it was the stout hearts and fighting spirit of the men who felt they sailed for sailors' rights, and who nurtured resentment over the British navy's treatment of sailormen. And it was the sailing skill of the captains and the lieutenants and the sailing quality of the design of old Joshua Humphreys, too. All these were a part of the story.

The British Admiralty could be forgiven for overlooking these factors in the heat of 1813 and 1814. The Admiralty, in its lordly fury, announced that hereafter, no British captain of a thirty-eight-gun frigate armed with eighteen-pounders was to engage an American frigate. That was like a small boy crying, "I won't fight you; you're too big for me," but it was necessary to reverse the whole tradition of the British navy after the Napoleonic wars were well begun: that a Nelson would fight anyone with anything.

The Admiralty wished to lose no more frigates in single battle, and so the order was issued, with the proviso that it could be overlooked if the action was unavoidable.

The British frigate captains were not pleased, by and large, with the checks placed on them. It was easy enough for the Admiralty to issue orders, it was something else again to sail a fine fighting ship and be told to stay away from an enemy of about your own size because he might whip you.

Ships of the line were to be cut down in the next few months, razeed, and then refitted to become two-deck vessels. That, said the Admiralty, was the reply to the American frigate.

Such attention paid to the little navy of the little country on the western shore of the Atlantic brought tremendous increase in prestige to the United States in the capitals of Europe. For the first time America was taken seriously; the courtiers in half a dozen countries decided that the Americans might possibly be there to stay. In London the *Times* took a very serious view of the American victories, particularly since, in the seven months of war, American ships had captured some five hundred British merchantmen, and then came these dreadful frigate fights — in which *not one* American ship was to strike her flag.

Equally important, at home, was the effect *Constitution* and the other frigates were having on morale. Early in January 1813, Congress had passed a bill authorizing the construction of four ships of the line and six more frigates. These would not see action in the War of 1812, but they were indicative of the new position of strength that the American navy would have.

When *Constitution* came home to Boston that February of 1813, she was suffering in places from rot in the timbers, as well as from her fight with *Java*. Rot would never do. In Britain some still said that the reason *Guerriere* was dismasted so quickly and her hull shot so full of holes could be attributed to rot. In any event, it was the sailor's enemy, and when discovered had best be dealt with rapidly. So *Constitution* went into the navy yard at Boston for a thorough overhaul. Commodore Bainbridge, suffering from his wounds, went off to recuperate and then to become commander of that very same navy yard. Captain Charles Stewart was made the new commander of *Constitution*. He was another of the mold of heroes, a boyhood friend and naval comrade of Stephan Decatur, a fighting sailor who had learned his trade under Captain Barry back before the turn of the century. He had fought the French and the Barbary pirates, and he knew what he was expected to do now — carry on the proud tradition of his service and his ship.

Stewart took over *Old Ironsides* on July 18, 1813. The whole crew had been paid off after the *Java* victory, and the officers scattered among other ships of the service. But Stewart had no trouble finding officers or crew for *Constitution*. Officers were eager to serve under him and aboard the vessel so renowned. Men from New England jammed the lists till none others need apply; *Connie* was a "lucky ship" in many a way. Had she not won her battles hands down with scarcely a man hurt or killed? Had she not won $100,000 for her crews in two engagements? By

151

midsummer Stewart had his complement, taking the pick of New England's finest sailors and fighting men.

And so, on December 30, *Old Ironsides* headed out to sea, to fight her country's enemies.

So adamant had the British government become that this troublesome war on the Atlantic be ended, that even sailing out was an adventure. The British had strengthened their squadrons on the American coast, blockading every major port with heavy vessels, those seventy-four-gun ships of the line and others that could outgun the frigates. So when Captain Stewart came out on December 30, he ran the British blockade, ready to pile on the canvas and run before a squadron, or fight a frigate if he found one.

Down went *Constitution*, sailing outside the coast, until she reached Guiana, where she searched for East Indiamen unsuccessfully and then turned toward the Windward Islands.

She began to have a little luck.

On February 14, 1814, the lookouts sighted a sail, and Captain Stewart ordered the chase to begin. After some time they overhauled a vessel, the ship *Lovel & Ann*, a British merchantman, which was captured. A prize crew was put aboard and she was sailed away, while *Constitution* continued her raiding.

The next day, the lookouts again sang out that a ship was approaching, and this time it turned out to be a proper warship, though a small one. *Constitution* ran her down, and found she was the

*Pictou*, a British war schooner. She was destroyed and her crew of seventy-five was captured.

Nine days later, Captain Stewart came upon the thirty-six-gun British frigate *La Pique* off Puerto Rico. Captain Maitland, the British commander was not looking for a fight with this famous ship. He recognized her as one of those dreaded American forty-fours that had Whitehall writing in excitement and issuing orders to beware — for the American vessels were not what they seemed to be. The warnings had taken effect with Captain Maitland; he consulted those orders that said he was not to engage a ship of the weight and gun of the *Constitution*, and he ran for it.

*La Pique* sailed well; the chase was hot, but when night fell and rain squalls pushed their way across the course, Captain Maitland managed to dodge into a cloud bank, and disappear in the darkness through Mona passage, and get clean away.

Such disappointments seemed the lot of *Constitution* and Captain Stewart on this voyage. Never had a commander and a crew sought glory more avidly. Never had they worked harder, or been of better spirit, confident and gleeful that they had their enemies on the run. And never had they shared so many disappointments. The log of the ship is filled with sightings and overhaulings — and the discovery that the ships they caught were Americans or neutrals and thus no game at all.

So the voyage went, with only a few prizes in the West Indies to assuage the thirst for glory. But not one grand encounter such as those of Hull and Bainbridge.

In March the ship headed north again, bound for Boston port and new orders that, hopefully, would take her into greater action. On April 2, the lookout sighted Portsmouth light off the coast, and they headed in to Portsmouth to anchor in a home port. But the wind shifted at sunrise on April 3, as they were making for the port, and Captain Stewart decided to head around and go into Boston instead.

He changed course, and at seven o'clock was Boston bound. Then the wind began to fail. By eight o'clock that morning it had hauled around to the north-northwest, and very nearly died on them. Just then, the lookouts spotted a pair of square-rigged vessels of good size on the southeast, coming up with the wind, which meant they had all the advantages if they were enemies. Captain Stewart first saw that they were men of war, by their bearing and those telltale ports, and he was quickly enough assured that they were enemy by their sails, and then by their colors.

Shades of Isaac Hull and the squadron that chased him off the Chesapeake! *Constitution*'s boards could not remember, but if they could, they would have seen that Captain Stewart was nearly in as desperate a position as had been Hull on that bad day. For the enemy had all the wind — coming up nicely on their breeze, sails filled and the white water lapping at their bows to show their speed, while where Stewart sat — and that is the word — scarcely a breath of air caught the outstretched canvas of old *Connie*.

Stewart was in familiar territory, about three miles east of Thacher's island. But to be becalmed here as he was for fully an hour was not anyone's idea of a fine day, particularly with those enemy ships coming up. They were typical British frigates, more heavily armed since the days of *Guerriere* and *Java*. If Stewart would have welcomed to fight one of them or both of them in turn, he would rather not chance the vessel to the pair in tandem. Two broadsides working him over, both ships in danger of taking him by raking; these were not ideas to contemplate with equanimity.

It was ten o'clock in the morning before that southeast breeze that he could see filling his enemy's sails began to come to him, and then he had the choice — he could tack down on the pair of them and fight. They would sail at him on the wind, probably one would pass down each side, and broadside him together as they passed. Or one might choose bow and one stern, and wear up and rake him, then go back on the wind and give him a broadside as they passed.

There was hardly choice here. Any sensible captain would run for it, and that is what Captain Stewart chose to do this morning. The enemy were scarcely three and a half miles away when *Constitution* caught the breeze.

Had there been a Salem man aboard the vessel, Captain Stewart might have run through the dangerous channel between Baker's Island and The Misery, but there was not, so Stewart headed around Halfway Rock, which meant he had plenty of water under his keel, but a round-about passage that might let the British cut him off.

In fifteen minutes it seemed certain that the British were still having all the best of the breeze, and they were gaining on *Constitution*. So Stewart decided to lighten ship. First went the spare spars — there were plenty of those in Boston Navy Yard if he were to be fortunate enough to see them there. Then went barrels of flour and pickles and molasses, until all but a handful of provisions were jettisoned. The bosun supervised the casting away of these valuables, and then reported back to the quarterdeck.

Still not enough. The enemy continued to run down on them. More must be given to the sea.

Prize goods, wonderful valuables from the ships they had captured, silks and brocades and silver and gold — these all went to Father Neptune's depths as well.

Captain Stewart looked grimly through the glass. Not yet enough.

They must start with the fresh water, and it was done. The pumps were put to the water room, and the casks pumped out and fresh became salt again, and the ship lightened.

Then came the unkindest blow of all. The grog

in the spirit room would have to go.

So the pumps were taken to the whiskey kegs and put in under the hard eye of officers who watched every spilled drop, and the precious life-giving fluid was pumped overboard as the men nearly wept. Then, certainly, they knew the depth of their danger.

The whiskey did it! In half an hour they were at least holding their own, and at noon *Constitution* rounded Halfway Rock, and set course for Marblehead harbor and safety.

In an hour she was able to anchor below Fort Sewall, while the British frigates stopped six miles away outside.

These ships were the *Tenedos* and the *Junon*, a part of one of the squadrons on blockade. Captain Parker of the *Tenedos* wanted to sail into Marblehead — he did not believe there were guns in that fort — and fight it out with the frigate in harbor. Captain Upton of the *Junon* overruled him.

Aboard *Constitution*, Captain Stewart was getting ready for what might come. He sent a boat ashore, and the militia — which meant every man who was able to bear a gun — was summoned to help fight at the fort and defend the ship in the harbor if need be.

Perhaps it was the sight of troops moving along the shore or the apparent rocklike settlement of *Constitution* before the fort, but the British gave up that afternoon and sailed away. And so at high water Captain Stewart took aboard a pilot named Captain Knott Martin, and sailed through the narrows and the treacherous shoal water to Salem and greater safety.

"I could have saved $10,000," he said to the pilot as they stood on the quarterdeck that afternoon, "if I had had you on board this morning."

For that was the value of the prize goods jettisoned.

To say nothing of the whiskey.

# CHAPTER SEVEN

## THE <u>CYANE</u> AND THE <u>LEVANT</u>

A few days after the narrow escape from the two British frigates off Marblehead, Captain Stewart took *Constitution* into Boston Harbor to repair the ravages of the chase. He slipped in quietly under cover, for the blockading British were more than a nuisance these days; they were downright dangerous and outside in such force that no frigate captain could feel safe.

Further, there was a new, if onerous duty to be performed.

The American merchant shipping bottled up in the harbor had to be protected from British raids. So *Constitution* was ordered to stay in port, and there to join the newly launched ship of the line *Independence* to guard against a British landing of troops bent on burning port and town. Commodore Bainbridge was in charge of this defense, and he wanted *Constitution* there to help him.

Other frigates were tied up in other places, doing the same task. *Constellation* sat in Norfolk harbor, and the *United States* was in New London.

Stewart insisted that he had the "right" to go out and fight if the conditions warranted, but the

British were good planners. There was only one real opportunity: if a storm smashed the port entrance so badly that visibility was cut to nothing and fighting was out of the question. But these conditions did not arise for Captain Stewart that spring or summer or fall. So *Constitution* sat in Boston harbor, waiting.

She was nearly lost to politicking in this time of American trouble. The people of Massachusetts, by and large, continued to oppose this War of 1812 that was playing havoc with their trade and their economy. They did not believe the federal government had the right to use state forces and state resources to carry the war except in protection of Massachusetts property. Indeed, at one point, they suggested that since there was danger of a British landing, and the ships *Constitution* and *Independence* would be major targets of the enemy, that the ships clear out of the inner harbor so nobody would get hurt when the British attacked them.

Bainbridge put a stern end to that — but the grumbling continued, and *Constitution* had little solace from the town in those hard days.

But they could not last forever.

The British, like everyone else, must eat and drink, and ship's rigging wore and sails became frayed in the constant rubbing of the winds. Most of the supply could be made by supply ships, but men could not remain at sea forever, nor could vessels. And when winter came, with its harsh storms over the northwest Atlantic, the

160

British seemed inclined to relax the blockade of Boston port. They moved offshore so as to be sure they had plenty of sea room in a driving wind. The blockade force consisted of a new fifty-gun frigate built especially to combat the American frigates, a forty-gun frigate, and an eighteen-gun brig. On December 12 they were all moving away from Boston harbor as *Constitution* was getting ready to make a run for the sea. Six days later, then, Captain Stewart did slip out, unnoticed, and soon cleared the land and headed southeast toward Bermuda to raid British merchant shipping and seek a naval battle if she could find one.

On Christmas Day, 1814, Captain Stewart came upon the British merchant brig *Lord Nelson*. The brig had run into trouble in the bad weather and could not keep up with the convoy of which she was a part. Lagging, she was captured, and then Captain Stewart had the problem, for his prize crew had the same trouble with the vessel. He took the ship in tow for a while and broke out the most valuable of the cargo, which was moved over to the frigate. Through some misunderstanding, Lieutenant William Taylor, the prize master, scuttled the ship — his orders had been to cut away her masts. So that was the end of that prize.

Finding little to interest her onshore, and in constant danger around the Americas from the heavily augmented British blockade forces, *Constitution* sailed eastward by way of Madeira to a position off the Portuguese coast. Here she might intercept British East Indiamen, who would not be expecting an American ship of war so far from home. These ships would not normally be escorted by war vessels of any kind. Britain ruled the waves, and there should be no reason for her merchantmen to be frightened on their own side of the Atlantic.

On February 18, 1815, Captain Stewart went after a sail, and soon enough discovered that the vessel was the bark *Julia*, sailing under the flag of the German state of Hamburg. From her captain, Stewart learned of the peace negotiations at Ghent. Late that day, stopping a Russian ship, he met two American ship captains traveling as passengers, who confirmed the reports and said the peace had actually been concluded, and the War of 1812 was ended.

This was all unofficial. Until he received official news of the war's end, Captain Stewart could do nothing but continue on a war basis. At least that is what he told himself, and he proceeded to search for British vessels. On February 17 he captured a British merchantman and sent her home under a prize crew. Whether or not the capture would stand up in court was debatable, but he was doing his duty.

All the talk about peace disturbed the eager young officers of the *Constitution* and the New England men who had signed on to secure some of that glory that rubbed off from her illustrious exploits of the war. Stewart was, to put it bluntly, itching for a fight, no matter what the state of the world at the moment. And one February day he told his officers that he had a presentiment: within a matter of hours they would meet the enemy and have their chance for glory.

If some of the British frigate captains had their way, it was certainly going to be the case. For many of these brave men, smarting under the defeats inflicted on them off the American coast, were ready to take up the gauntlet and seek honor at any time. Frigate captains always seemed to regard their vessels as weapons of chivalry, and war as a matter of dueling among equals. But that was the temper of the times, and was already changing in the system of blockade squadrons, convoys, and armored ships to come. With each technical advancement of naval warfare the rules were changed and the aspects of chivalry moved further back into the distance.

This February — as Captain Stewart was moving about off the Portuguese shore and deciding to head for Madeira again, in search of his combat — an old enemy of *Constitution* was abroad. Captain Dacres, who had commanded the *Guerriere* in that famous battle with *Old Ironsides*, had a new British frigate, the *Tiber*, and he was still as eager as ever to contest the sea with *Constitution*. To his dying day he would claim that the victory of Isaac Hull over him so many months before had been largely a matter of luck. One of the ships that Stewart had chased came into Lisbon, where Dacres' vessel was anchored, and her captain reported on the pursuit by a big American frigate, that Dacres recognized as *Old Ironsides* or one of her class. So he set out immediately to give chase and scoured the area where the big merchantman had been pursued.

By this time, however, Captain Stewart was on his way toward Madeira, so Dacres had to give up in despair, while Captain Stewart headed westward, secure in his belief that he was going into action.

At noon on February 20, *Old Ironsides* was sailing along briskly under full canvas, in a following wind that settled down to become a light easterly breeze. Madeira was about one hundred eighty miles to the southwest of her.

At one o'clock a sail was sighted on the port bow and Captain Stewart set off in pursuit, making every bit of sail the frigate could carry. An hour later the foretop lookout reported a second sail, in line with the first, but beyond it.

From the deck of *Constitution* as the hull of the first ship appeared above the horizon, she seemed to be a ship of the line, for the men thought they counted three tiers of ports on her. She was actually the British frigate *Cyane*, under Captain Gordon Thomas Falcon. Beyond her, not yet recognizable at the moment, was the sloop *Levant*, under Captain George Douglas. They were on their way from Gibraltar to the West Indies, and they were keeping their eye out for *Constitution*, having heard that she had been sighted between Madeira and the coast of Portugal.

Stewart and his officers trod their quarterdeck and they talked as they waited to overhaul the other vessel.

Was it wise to take on so large a ship? asked the lieutenant cautiously.

Stewart thought so. The vessel ahead of them did not look by her canvas and her set to be as large as those portholes would suggest. Had not the lieutenant heard of false ports, that little bit of psychological warfare?

"Be this as it may, you know I promised you a fight before the setting of today's sun," Stewart added, "and if we do not take it now that it is offered, we can scarcely have another chance. We must flog them when we catch them, whether she has one gun-deck or two."

*Constitution* drove down on them then, as good as Stewart's word, with the wind coming fair, and the studding sails bellied out, nicely canted and taking the breeze in that fine way she had of doing it.

Through the glasses Stewart and his officers saw action aboard the other ships, little dots moving about the decks, the glint of a port opening here and there, and frantic movement of signal flags that meant the two captains were conferring. They must be talking about their course of action now.

*Cyane* was indeed calling upon *Levant* to come up and confer; Captain Falcon wanted to make a battle plan with Captain Douglas.

All this was observed from the rail and hammock nets of *Constitution* as she sailed on down wind, making her twelve knots and more in the gathering breeze.

Then there came an ominous cracking sound.

Looking up, Captain Stewart saw his main royal mast breaking away, at the eyes of the topgallant rigging. They had those sails so extended and pulling so hard that this piece of wood had weakened and given away.

So it was up the futtocks for the top hands, dropping a line and bringing up a new royal spar, and fastening it and cutting and splicing and tying together the rigging, so that the sails could be remounted and begin driving once again.

All this while the other canvas had held up, and Stewart had no thought of slacking sail for the repairs. In the fifteen minutes they took, he watched anxiously, but no, the other vessels were not drawing away; he was holding his own, and when the mast was up, through the glass he could see that he was gaining .

The day was waning. It was now five o'clock in the afternoon. From Stewart's point of view it was a beautiful chase, for he had the wind and he was overhauling his enemies, and there was time to fight. He ordered the gunners of the bow chasers to begin laying their pieces, and tried a few shots at the frigate before him, but they all fell short. The distance was yet too great

The two British ships joined, and hauled on

the starboard tack, trying to come around and get to windward of the *Constitution* as good fighting technique demanded. Apparently — or so Stewart believed — the British captains would prefer to delay the action until night. By getting the wind gauge, they hoped to come up and cripple their opponent under cover of darkness.

For Captain Falcon, the decision to fight the big American frigate was a difficult one. For his ship was really more a corvette than a frigate. In spite of all those gunports, she carried only thirty-four guns and one hundred eighty men, and was in no way equal to *Constitution*. The brig was even smaller, but the captains were brave men, and they had a good reason to fight: two important convoys of merchant ships had recently sailed from Gibraltar, and Falcon hoped by disabling *Constitution*, to keep her from interfering with them.

Together, the British ships stripped down their running canvas and made ready to begin the fight. *Levant* was ahead, with *Cyane* two hundred yards astern.

*Constitution* bore down on them with the wind, which was over her port quarter, and stripped down her upper canvas so it might not get in the way in the tacking Captain Stewart expected to be doing as they fought.

At 6:10 *Cyane* was on the port quarter and *Levant* on the port bow. Captain Stewart ordered the gunners to open fire. The broadsides began, every gun on the *Constitution* firing as she came into position. The British gunners replied, and a cloud of smoke began to rise between the vessels.

For fifteen minutes it was shot and shot, at the end of that time Stewart ordered his men to cease firing because his guns and the enemy's had completely covered the ships by smoke — sails and all — and he had to find the enemy once more before he began wasting ammunition instead of sending it home.

Now darkness had fallen and the moon had come up, as the smoke drifted downwind from the quiet scene, the silence punctuated only by an occasional gunshot and the creaking of the rigging of the ships.

As the smoke cleared, Stewart found *Constitution* was abreast of the smaller *Levant*, while *Cyane* was luffing up astern in hopes of delivering a raking broadside to dismast or cripple the big frigate.

Stewart assessed the situation.

"Fire," he shouted to the gunners to port, and a broadside rang out against the side of *Levant*, the guns double shotted this time.

Immediately, Stewart ordered his main and mizzent topsails back and loosed the foresails, so that they shook in the breeze.

*Constitution* moved straight backwards then, stern on, across the bow of the *Cyane*, and instead of Captain Falcon raking *Constitution*, Stewart raked *Cyane* from bow to stern and forced her to bear off and keep away. It was a remarkable display of seamanship and military judgment.

*Levant* moved to come back to help *Cyane*, but in a moment, the yards were turned and caught the wind. The sails filled, and *Constitution* shot ahead in the breeze and fired two broadsides into the stern of *Levant* as she was trying to turn.

Captain Falcon now came to the rescue of the smaller ship, and stood in between *Levant* and *Constitution*, while Captain Douglas moved away, his rigging badly cut up and ship sorely hurt.

*Cyane* was in the middle. Captain Falcon tried to go off before the wind, but *Constitution* moved and gave her a raking fire again, with such deadly effect that the men of the *Cyane* were driven momentarily from their guns and could not fire.

*Cyane* moved around and fired her port battery into the starboard bow of *Constitution*.

It was now 6:50 and the moon was shining as they fought, the blasts from the gun muzzles showing red and the smoke drifting up to pass away in the moonlight.

*Levant* was moving away, sheeting up her topgallant sails, *Cyane* was stunned, trying to move away. *Constitution* had the wind and moved up beside her, ready to deliver another big broadside. *Constitution* stood on the port quarter of *Cyane*, the British ship's guns would not train on the American, and the *Cyane* was virtually at the mercy of Captain Stewart.

Captain Falcon saw his situation. He fired a gun to leeward and sent a man into the rigging with a light that was a token of surrender. To fight on might be suicidal. His ship had been hulled several times and was leaking badly. A number of the carronades on the forecastle and quarterdeck had broken loose and were more dangerous to the men on deck than any number of American shot or blasts of grape. His rigging was shot up badly, so much so that the main and mizzenmasts hung drunkenly, and threatened to go over the side with any undue motion. Of her crew of one hundred eighty, twelve men were dead and twenty-six injured, and in Captain Falcon's opinion the difference between surrender now and later was that he would now surrender a ship, and later give up a worthless hulk.

So the surrender was made. Lieutenant B. V. Hoffman of *Constitution* took a boat and crew to *Cyane*, and took charge there.

*Constitution* had no time to stop at the moment; Captain Stewart still had to deal with *Levant*, which had seemed to be fleeing, but which was actually moving away only to repair rigging so that her captain could come back and fight for Falcon once again.

It was 8:50 that night, however, before the two ships edged warily up to one another, and it was obvious that it would be a most unequal battle. For *Levant* mounted but twenty-one guns, eighteen short thirty-two-pounders that were good for close work but no good to stand off and pound away against twenty-four-pounder long guns.

Nonetheless, the fight was joined. *Levant* passed to leeward of *Constitution* and they exchanged broadsides. That first exchange showed Captain Douglas what he was up against, and seeing that his fellow ship had run down her colors and there was nothing to be gained by trying to help her now, he put on all canvas and tried to make a run. It was going to be hard. His wheel had been shot away and that last broadside had done much damage aloft.

Captain Stewart saw it all by the light of that moon, and wore *Constitution* around to chase. The smaller ship moved out, but by 9:30 *Constitution* was in close pursuit, and sending shots from her long bow guns into the fleeing English vessel. Seeing, hearing, and knowing what must come, Captain Douglas hauled down his flag, as the Yankees gave a cheer.

On the deck of *Constitution*, John Lancey of Cape Ann was dying of his wounds, and he heard and waved the stump of his arm and tried to join in the cheer as the surgeon worked over him. Then he stopped suddenly — and died.

All in all, *Constitution* lost six killed and nine wounded, not bad for a double fight, most of it by moonlight.

In the past the stories told about the battles had indicated the highest good will between the men of the two navies once the shot stopped falling and the colors were withdrawn. But not this day. Perhaps it was the changing face of war, but after this battle the British prisoners broke into the grog room of their ships, and into the store-rooms of *Cyane* and pillaged what they would. They complained thereafter that they were in turn pillaged by the Americans, and Stewart ordered a careful investigation of the duffel of all his men, to find very little that was contraband.

In the wardroom of the *Constitution* the two British captains seemed inclined to refight the battle over the port bottle, and got into so brisk an argument as to which of them had failed in tactics and seamanship that Captain Stewart felt impelled to intervene, and to offer to fight the whole battle over again if they so wished it.

But as all this went on, *Constitution*'s men were working briskly and with a will, preparing their three ships for sea. They overhauled and repaired the spars of the two prizes, which were badly injured by round shot and grape.

The next day, Captain Stewart considered his course. He was deep in the waters frequented by the enemy, and if he was to get these ships to a neutral port, where the prize money could be claimed, he must move swiftly and accurately. He could head for Madeira, but he decided instead to run for the Cape Verde Islands, because he would have less chance of encountering a British force en route.

So that is the course he followed, sailing for Porto Prayo on the island of St. Jago. They sailed, and they arrived on March 10, 1815. They found an English brig and hired it to serve as a ship for the prisoners, who must be returned home. A hundred of the prisoners were put on board to get the brig ready for sea, and the others were landed in a day or so.

Fog set in, and this delayed all the work, so that on March 12 they were still in port when the upper sails of a large ship were seen in the fog.

One of the English midshipmen saw the vessels first, and he reported as a matter of curiosity to Lieutenant Shubrick, the officer of the deck of the *Constitution*. It was just about noon, when an excited Shubrick burst into Captain Stewart's cabin with the breathless information that they might be in deep trouble. For the first sail had been joined by two more, and it seemed they were standing in for the port.

Stewart was not unduly worried at the first report — he intended to raise anchor and go out and take a look at the stranger. But when the amplification came, with word of two more ships, he was sure they were English men of war, and that meant the end of him if he were caught. So he ordered the cables slipped, ready to sacrifice the anchor, and signaled to *Cyane* and *Levant* that they, too, were to get under way.

In fifteen minutes *Constitution* was standing out to sea, under her topsails, followed by the prizes. The Portuguese batteries opened up on the ships as they left — that was an indication of the Portuguese governor's feeling toward the Americans, and ample justification for Stewart's unease. No damage was done, but the ships outside were warned of a crisis of some kind and were very watchful.

As they cleared the port, more canvas went up aboard *Constitution* and her prizes — and a good thing, for the English vessels (which indeed they were) had now become thoroughly excited, and they began to chase. Stewart could see only the sails of the other ships, but from these he deduced that he faced two ships of the line and a frigate. He ordered his men to cut away the cutter and gig that were still dragging at the stern, so quickly had they left the port.

And then they came close enough that several of the officers among the English prisoners could recognize the ships, the squadron of Sir George Ralph Collier, consisting of the fifty-gun frigates *Leander* and *Newcastle*, both outclassing *Constitution*, and the forty-gun frigate *Acasta*.

The British ships were beating up against the breeze, and the *Constitution* and her prizes came out on the east side of the harbor, to windward of their enemy. They were lucky, the wind saved them without a doubt. Sailing under topsails, they managed to avoid detection until they cleared the point, and raised all sail — which was immediately spotted by the British lookouts.

What an irony — for this squadron had been stationed on the American coast, and had come across the sea in pursuit of *Constitution*, chasing all the way after *Old Ironsides* had made her escape from the blockade of Boston. Captain Collier had the distinct impression that there were three American frigates — *President, Congress,* and *Constitution* all together, and so now even though he saw three vessels, he was very cautious in his approach. His two big ships might technically outgun the Americans, but if those three frigates were traveling together, there was going to be one grand fight.

When discovered, *Constitution* was only a mile ahead of her enemies, all six ships on the port tack, lying close to the wind. They were after *Constitution* as soon as they recognized her.

At 12:50 *Newcastle* and *Leander* were on the lee quarter of *Constitution,* and *Cyane* was falling back so far that her capture seemed imminent. Stewart ordered Lieutenant Hoffman to tack north and west — he did, and was soon out of the way altogether as the British continued to chase *Old Ironsides.* Then *Levant* began to fall back; Stewart ordered her to tack away, and once more the British ships kept after *Constitution. Levant* made it clear until she was lost from view.

At 1:45 the British captains felt close enough that they opened fire on *Constitution* with their chase guns. They were not close enough; the shots fell off, but they were so close that the officers could see one another upon their quarter-decks, and standing on the hammock nettings.

*Levant* now came back into view, causing some confusion. Stewart ordered her away again, at three o'clock, as the British seemed to be gaining on him too, and he ordered her to tack away, which she did. Then all three British ships tacked after *Levant,* leaving *Constitution* quite alone, sailing merrily away from them. Poor *Levant* was to be the sacrifical lamb as it turned out — here were three big British frigates chasing one small ship, which they improperly identified as an American frigate.

They chased her back into Porto Praya, and she anchored with all dignity, whereupon these three behemoths surrounded her, assisted by British sailors who had been ashore (and who had manned those Portuguese guns to fire against *Constitution* when she went out). Then the British frigates — all three of them fired broadside after broadside at *Levant* without hitting her once. Finally Lieutenant Ballard of *Constitution,* the prize master, became afraid that somebody might get hurt and being in the position that he was, he hauled down Old Glory and the *Levant* was returned to her original owners.

Meanwhile, *Constitution* was long gone, and the three British frigate commanders were in harbor with what a later generation would call "egg on their face." What an embarrassment. The justification of it made to the Admiralty was that the commanders expected to find three big American fighting ships, and when they had chased them in the bad weather they were sure that was what they were chasing.

*Newcastle* and *Acasta* seemed to have even worse vision than that indicated on the day they fought with *Levant* in the harbor. They kept firing after the flag came down, and when they eventually came aboard, they were certain that they were on the American sloop *Hornet*.

*Cyane*, which had tacked away, obedient to Stewart's orders early in the chase, reached New York on April 10, and *Constitution* sailed to Brazil to land prisoners. Only then did Captain Stewart begin to piece together the story of *Levant* and his own narrow escape became even narrower. Soon he headed north, and stopped off at Puerto Rico, where Stewart learned that the war with Britain was indeed over. Then he set sail for home port — Boston — arriving there on May 16, 1815. The most famous frigate in American history had fought her last battle.

# CHAPTER EIGHT

## AY, TEAR THE TATTERED
## ENSIGN DOWN ...

The War of 1812 ended; *Constitution* was laid up for repairs. Once again she was suffering from the endemic disease of wooden ships: rot. Thus, when the troubles with the Barbary pirates broke out, and Stephen Decatur was sent to quell them, with one squadron, and Bainbridge with another, *Old Ironsides* was left behind. As affairs turned out, it was six years before she was needed again and was commissioned to sail under Captain Jacob Jones as flagship of the Mediterranean squadron.

It was like the old days: she sailed to Gibraltar in twenty-one days, and then began a cruise of the Mediterranean. Lord Byron visited the ship. She called at several ports and was treated like the queen she was.

She was active then for the next few years, back to Boston for an eager young crew, out again to the Mediterranean under Captain Thomas Macdonough this time. Then came a succession of captains and assignments as *Old Ironsides* stood sentinel in the Mediterranean, reminding the world that American might crossed the Atlantic and particularly reminding those troublesome men of Barbary of their treaty obligations.

In these years of peace, as the old wooden ships came back to port and were surveyed by the naval architects, most of the warships of the War of 1812 were broken up or sold off. In 1828 the surveyors looked over *Constitution*, and decided that she was unfit and that it would be wise to break her up and build an entirely new ship. So the Navy Department decided this was the thing to do.

The news spread through Boston, and many citizens were shocked because here was Boston's very own ship, manned many a time by Massachusetts and, in all, the most heroic ship of the American navy.

A young student named Oliver Wendell Holmes heard of this plan, and he was so upset he sat down and wrote a poem. He sent it to the Boston *Advertiser*, which published the poem on September 16, 1830.

"*Old Ironsides*" it was called, and it became a famous poem, copied by newspapers all over the country, helping to make the reputation of this young man who would later become one of America's renowned poets, as well as an essayist and novelist:

Ay tear her tattered ensign down!
   Long has it waved on high,
And many an eye has danced to see
   That banner in the sky:

Beneath it rung the battle shout,
    And burst the cannon's roar;
The meteor of the ocean air
    Shall sweep the clouds no more.

Her deck, once red with heroes' blood,
    Where knelt the vanquished foe,
When winds were hurrying o'er the flood,
    And waves were white below,
No more shall feel the victor's tread,
    Or know the conquered knee;
The harpies of the shore shall pluck
    The eagle of the sea.

Oh, better that her shattered bulk
    Should sink beneath the wave;
Her thunders shook the mighty deep,
    And there should be her grave;
Nail to the mast her holy flag,
    Set every threadbare sail.
And give her to the god of storms,
    The lightning and the gale!

What a commotion the poem did cause. It was reprinted time and again, handbills were made of it to be passed along the streets of Washington, where Congressmen would see them.

The effect was electric. Congress stirred. The Navy Department revoked the order that the ship was to be destroyed. She would be rebuilt.

And that she was. On June 24, 1833, Captain Isaac Hull once more took command of his favorite ship, and directed the docking of *Old Iron-sides* in the new dry dock at Boston Navy Yard. A huge crowd watched, a crowd led by Vice-President Martin Van Buren, and including notables from all the New England states.

So *Old Ironsides* was restored.

She had new guns. She had new timbers and new decking and everything she needed to be the queen ship of the navy. She even had a new figurehead.

Captain Jesse D. Elliott, the commander of the Boston Navy Yard in the spring of 1833, decided to replace the billethead with a figurehead of President Andrew Jackson, who had just then completed a visit to Boston in which he was welcomed as hero.

What an error!

Andrew Jackson, since the days of the War of 1812, had become a political figure and most controversial. He was a Democrat; the Whigs of Boston rose up, claiming that a national patriotic symbol was being turned to party politics.

And indeed there seemed to be something to this for Elliott *was* a Jacksonian Democrat. With this uproar, it seemed obvious that he would back down and retrieve the old nonpolitical figurehead or have another made which would not be controversial. But Elliott insisted on the head being finished and placed aboard the ship in the spring of 1834.

The precautions that were taken would fill a book. The ship was moored between ships of the line for safety, a marine guard was stationed so that she could be seen from any angle, and the guard around the yard was more than doubled.

It was a handsome figurehead, a full-length figure of that leonine Andrew Jackson, the heroic general of the Battle of New Orleans, dressed in formal clothes with a cloak around his shoulders, holding the manuscript of a statesman.

The more the political enemies of Jackson saw it, the more they were infuriated, just as the more Captain Elliott and the friends of Jackson saw it, the more they were pleased.

In that summer of 1834, passions were high; *Constitution* became a political symbol, and the enemies of Jackson were joined by many businessmen and conservatives who felt it was improper for living political figures to be honored by such representations.

Among these dissenters were a pair of Boston businessmen, brothers and shipowners named Henry and William Lincoln. They owned a number of vessels trading in the West Indies.

One day they were in their countinghouse when the young captain in their employment came in, on leave between voyages to the Indies. He was Samuel W. Dewey, son of an officer who had once commanded Fort Independence, and nephew of a former postmaster of New York. He was a well-to-do young man, a bit on the harum-scarum side, as they said in Boston, but a competent captain for all that, and well regarded by the Lincolns.

They passed the time of day and gossiped a bit about public affairs. And as such things would happen, the conversation turned to the Andrew Jackson figurehead that had so recently been installed aboard *Old Ironsides*.

It was an outrage to the people of Boston, the commonwealth of Massachusetts, and to America, to see the grand old ship disfigured thus, said William Lincoln.

Then why not do something about it, said Captain Dewey.

Because the ship was so heavily guarded by Captain Elliott's men, said Merchant Lincoln.

"I would give a hundred dollars to see that figurehead cut off," he said, as Captain Dewey bid him good day and waved his way out of the countinghouse.

Some time passed, Captain Dewey's ship was delayed, and he decided he would try to collect the "bet" from William Lincoln. The idea of taking off the figurehead appealed to his youthful sense of daring.

Captain Dewey watched the weather. On the night of July 2 came the kind of an evening he had been waiting for. He laid on a small boat, took it down to the Charles River across from the navy yard, and as dusk fell he went down to the boat with a saw, two gimlets, and a piece of light line. He looked upward — the weather was sufficiently forbidding, and soon it must break into a thunderstorm. Anyone with any sense would be staying close to cover on a night like this one.

In the darkness, Captain Dewey rowed across the Charles, and pulled up alongside the *Independence*, one of the ships of the line that were guarding *Old Ironsides* and her new figurehead. At the gangway he stopped, secured his tools around him, and worked his little boat around the timbers of the big ship until he reached the gangway of *Constitution*. Then, silently, he climbed upward.

It was pitch dark, raining, and there was not a guard in sight. He made his way to the bowsprit and climbed out under it, facing the figurehead. He screwed a gimlet into each side of Andy Jackson's head and passed a line over the bowsprit to make it fast to both of the gimlets.

Then he lay on his back, directly under the figure, and with his saw began to cut away — under cover of the thunder and the rain.

The first cut struck a bolt. He had to start all over again. Finally he did it — he cut through, and the head hung down by the gimlets on the line. Swiftly and quietly he brought the head of the president down into the boat, which was now half full of water because he had been so unwise as to leave it under the scupper drainage and *Old Ironsides* had filled his boat up for him as he worked. But not quite is not the same as sunk, and bailing a little and rowing very carefully, he managed the crossing of the Charles in the rainstorm, and stowed his trophy in a coffee bag and carried it through the streets to his mother's house, on Pearl Street, where he hid it in a sea chest.

Morning came on July 3, and with it the workers and change of guard. Someone noticed that Andy Jackson had lost his head in the night, and then there was a hullaballoo! The police were called. The people shouted on the dock-yard — what they shouted depended on which side they favored, the pro-Jackson side or the anti-Jacksonians.

Captain Elliott was furious and immediately sent off a message to the Secretary of the Navy demanding a full investigation and prosecution of the offenders for destroying government property.

While this consternation raged at the navy yard, the Lincoln brothers went to their count-inghouse as usual, and on that morning of July 3 they had a call from young Captain Dewey. He had the head, he said, and Mr. Lincoln owed him a hundred dollars.

When the news reached Washington, one re-acted on the basis of his political tenets. Such charges as "treason" filled the air, and Jacksonian congressmen fulminated that the man who had mutilated an American warship must be punished.

But young Captain Dewey never was punished. Within a day or two everyone in Boston knew what he had done, and that the head was somewhere around the city. Yet he remained free. The "crime" was political to some and a prank to others, but the wise heads in Boston and Washington knew that to try to punish it would be to create a political trial that might backfire against the Jackson Democrats and the navy.

Captain Dewey became quite a celebrity for a time. He had the picture of a saw printed on the back of his greeting cards. He never made any denials that he had done the cutting, and about six months later he gave the head to the Secretary of the Navy.

Captain Elliott brooded for a while over the insults, but finally all quieted down. And when it did, and *Constitution* was ready to go to sea and active duty again in the winter of 1834-35, he had her ordered down to New York. In March, 1835, he sailed her down there himself, and brought the original carver of the Jackson figurehead down to the city to repair the damage. The carver, Mr. L. S. Beecher, fashioned a new head to fit the body, and it was repaired as cunningly as the artists and artisans could do it. So *Old Ironsides* went to sea again with Andy Jackson at her bow, and sailed with that figurehead for forty years, until it was removed and secured at the United States Naval Academy.

*Old Ironsides* was back in service. She did many a job for Americans in these peaceful years, and for a time Captain Elliott was her commander, and more, commander-in-chief of the Mediterranean squadron. He took ministers to their posts, and made calls of honor on many ports; she visited Constantinople and Marseille and

Malta and Le Havre and Plymouth. He fired her guns to salute royalty and other ships and on national holidays — but never in anger, for America was at peace with all the world. She entered and enjoyed many a port with British vessels that had tried in times past to catch her and blow her out of the water. But times had changed, no longer were American seamen bothered by British impressment; in foreign ports Americans and British even went out together.

In the summer of 1838 *Old Ironsides* came home again after a long, if uneventful, stay abroad. Captain Elliott left her — under a cloud, in fact — for in addition to being the most political figure ever to have trod *Old Ironsides'* deck as captain, he was also the harshest disciplinarian. He might have done well in the British navy in the days of Captain Bligh. He did so badly in the American navy in the postwar years, that he was found guilty of extreme harshness and suspended from his commission for four years.

*Old Connie* survived Captain Elliott as she had survived many another disaster in her day. On March 1, 1839, she was recommissioned at the Norfolk navy yard and, spick and span, she sailed as flagship for Commodore Alexander Claxton's squadron on a voyage to the South Pacific, a voyage of discovery and show the flag, and one most notable for the death of Commodore Claxton from illness while on board. He was succeeded in command by Captain Daniel Turner, who brought *Old Ironsides* back to Norfolk in the fall of 1841.

In 1843 and 1844 she was again on active service and for a few months was under her old commander Charles Stewart, who had progressed in the navy to become a commodore and had a squadron of his own. Then a famous captain named "Mad Jack" Percival took *Old Ironsides* to China by way of Rio de Janeiro where they dropped off the new America minister. Around the Cape of Good Hope they went and to Singapore, where the Americans encountered another old acquaintance — Henry D. Chads, the lieutenant of the *Java* who had taken command in the middle of the fight against *Old Ironsides*. Chads was now a commodore, and he came to the rescue of the men of the American frigate. Unused to the malarial climates of the east, they were coming down sick by the score in Singapore, and half the crew was unfit for duty when Commodore Chads sent his medical officers aboard to teach the Americans how they must live in this climate. Chads himself came for a visit, and sat in the wardroom where he had lamented as a prisoner so many years before, and told stories of the famous battle that *Constitution* and her men had won from him.

In the spring and summer of 1845 *Constitution* sailed about the eastern seas, visiting Canton and Manila and many a port between. In September she was in Honolulu, and in December she rounded Cape Horn and came home, again by way of Rio de Janeiro. These were long voyages for the old frigate — she used 500 gallons of fresh water a day and had to ship enough for 61 days from Rio to Boston port, where she arrived on September 28, 1846, after a cruise of 52,279 miles and 495 days at sea.

For two more years she sat in harbor, and then was taken to Europe on a cruise as flagship of a new touring squadron under Commodore W. C. Bolton. She was out of commission in 1851 in New York, and went back to the Mediterranean in December 1852. But *Constitution*'s days as an active warship were now nearing their end because steam was beginning to crowd the sailing vessels. She had one more spurt of honor and glory, as a chase ship off Africa in the suppression of the slave trade on the route between Cape Verde and St. Helena. She captured but one slaver in all that time, the American schooner *H. N. Gambrill*, but that was not an accurate record of her adventures. The trouble was several fold:

1. The slave ships were sleek and small and fast.

2. The slavers had become very cautious and moved off the normal shipping lanes to sneak back and forth across the ocean.

3. The trade to the Caribbean and to the North American shore was heavily suppressed by the rise of Abolitionism, and similar feelings in the Caribbean. The trade ships into South

America avoided the lanes that *Constitution* frequented.

4. Most ships carried foreign papers — perhaps several sets of them — and Brazilian and Portuguese and Spanish were the most common. Americans hesitated sometimes to take such ships, because of the international implications.

So *Connie* had adventures in the slave trade that were far more exciting than her logbook would indicate.

But then in 1855 the adventures came to an end. Steam had done its job, and she was taken out of commission at Portsmouth, New Hampshire. That was the end of her active service as a warship.

# EPILOGUE

In the first hundred years of the Republic, Americans were so busy creating a new society and the sinews of the nation that they had little time to consider history. Buildings, ships, and many a historic site were obliterated in this never-ending search for the better place and the better way. So *Constitution* was lucky, far more than many another vessel, in that she was saved from destruction in the critical years.

Part of it, of course, was the residue of sentiment shown in Oliver Wendell Holmes' famous poem. Those who suggested that *Old Ironsides* be allowed to rot away or be destroyed were quelled before the suggestion ever left Washington. But part of the reason for her happy survival was a need for her, even after the days of sail were giving away to steam. In the late 1850s steam was still not widely trusted or trustworthy, so most steamers carried canvas and masts and yards. The canvas could be spread to help the ship along in a good wind, or to supplant the steam plant if it should break down, which happened from time to time.

Even on these hermaphrodite ships, then, naval men must learn the old ways of life before the mast and seamanship, and young officers must be proficient in both forms, sail and steam. So *Old Ironsides*, in 1860, was commissioned as a

191

naval training vessel and sent down to the naval academy at Annapolis under Commander David D. Porter, on August 1.

Then came the election of Abraham Lincoln to the presidency, the secession of the Southern states, and the beginning of the Civil War at Fort Sumter.

*Connie* was in danger, and there was no doubt about it.

The frigate *United States* had been at Norfolk when the war broke, and she was burned to prevent capture. In the hands of an enemy, *Constitution* could once again become a formidable weapon (as the adventures of the raider *Alabama* indicated), and the naval authorities at Washington were worried.

On April 21, 1861, the navy ordered Lieutenant George W. Rodgers to move *Constitution* away from her berth at Annapolis harbor and out into the open roads, ready to go to sea. As *Old Ironsides* was making ready to weigh anchor, the steamer *Maryland* arrived in the harbor, carrying a regiment of Massachusetts volunteer soldiers, under the command of Brigadier General Benjamin F. Butler. How appropriate it was for them, men from *Constitution*'s home state, to guard her and help the midshipmen and sailors take her out to sea.

But it was not going to be so easy as all that. A good number of midshipmen had left the academy and gone home to join the Southern war effort. So had some of the officers. *Constitu-*

*tion* was in the hands of amateurs now, not the old sailing men of the days of Hull and Stewart. She slipped her moorings, except the starboard bow anchor, and was taken in tow by the *Maryland*. And the *Maryland* seemed to be in the hands of amateurs as well, for off Greenbury's Point, she cut in too close to land, and put *Constitution* "on the beach," stuck firmly aground. Working around, to try to get the frigate off, *Maryland* ran aground round on the other side of the channel.

What a mess it was!

The tide was racing out that night as the ships stuck tight. But the officers and men of the navy contingent and the army could not stop. They had heard a rumor that the Confederates would come up and try to mine the channel that night, so they *must* get these ships off and out to safety.

The men of *Old Ironsides* took a page from Isaac Hull's musty log of so many years ago. She had been kedged so well then, she might be kedged again — and that is the course they chose. They brought her boats and the boats of *Maryland*, and every other boat they could find in the area, and they pulled her off with the first run-out of the kedge. Then up came a squall, and drove her into the mud once more.

At about this time, off to seaward, the sailors of *Constitution* spotted several ships, steamers and sailing vessels. Was this the Confederate force that expected to come up that night to block Annapolis harbor? *Constitution*, reduced to a training ship, was no longer in condition to make a fight.

But there was no need. The ships in sight were carrying New York troops for the Union forces, and they were soon landed inshore, to guard against Southern takeover of the capital of Maryland.

*Constitution* got out of the mud and was towed into deep water and soon moved on up to New York Navy Yard.

Back at Annapolis, the war scare continued, and in Washington the Navy Department decided that the academy must be moved for the duration to a port much more definitely inside Union territory. So Newport, Rhode Island, was chosen as the wartime training center, and the midshipmen moved up there as quickly as the change could be made. *Constitution* left New York and joined them there, to remain until August, 1865, when she again went to Annapolis, sailing her way down. It was as if those old timbers had a life of their own this day, for *Constitution* beat her own sailing records, and managed for several hours to log 13.5 knots!

In these postwar days all the important figures of the navy trod her decks at one time or another, and for three years she was commanded by the officer who would go down in history as Admiral George Dewey, the hero of Manila bay and the Spanish-American War.

But now they let her go to pieces. By 1871 a survey party found her unfit for sea. Neglect had wrecked her yards and rotted her canvas and the timbers of her hull. She was scheduled to be moved to Philadelphia, and it was decided that she was unfit to be sailed up, so she had the ignominy of being towed all the way outside and up the Delaware. Sad day indeed for the mighty frigate that she once was. Would there be another Oliver Wendell Holmes to save her, as it seemed there must? Indeed someone even suggested that she be converted to a steam vessel!

But wise heads saved her once again. Congress and the navy men spoke up for her historic significance and the pride men could find in her and in their country through her story. She was rebuilt — hopefully to be exhibited in the Centennial exhibition of Liberty at Philadelphia in 1876 — but she was not ready in time.

What a change the builders made in her. They put in steam heat for the convenience of the officers and crew — and, of course, that "improvement" changed her altogether from the sturdy vessel of hardy sailing men. But these were modern times and few seemed to see the anomaly of the changes. She was commissioned again in July, 1877, really as an oddity. In 1878, she was sent to carry goods to the Universal Exposition at Paris.

The changes made in *Constitution* to make a cargo carrier of her turned out to be a serious mistake. On the voyage to Le Havre her timbers began to loosen, and by the time she got there she was taking water in a serious way, and had to be reworked in dock while she waited there for the exposition to end and the materials to be brought back to her.

There she sat, the black-hulled frigate with that broad band of white that outlined the main deck, reminder of the grand old days of sail. She received as much attention from travelers as many exhibits up there in Paris.

On the way home from Le Havre, *Constitution* had more bad luck — she ran aground on the second night out, and was stuck on Ballard's Point near Swanage on the English coast. It took five tugs to get her off into deep water, and then she had to put in at Portsmouth for repairs. The British navy, remembering the reputation of the fine old fighting ship, turned every effort to do a first-class job of repair in little time. Then off she went again on a stormy January day, and was hit by a gale, which caused the rudder to be twisted completely off. Captain O. C. Badger then accomplished a remarkable feat of seamanship in running before the gale, steering largely with the sails, and reaching Lisbon and safety. The repairs this time were longer in the making, and it was May 24, 1879, before the famous frigate sailed into New York harbor.

The Navy men who had served aboard *Constitution* as midshipmen wanted to keep the glorious old ship in service, so they now turned her over to a training school for apprentice seamen, and for the next two years she was cruising fruitfully from the West Indies to Halifax, much as she had done in the days of the French troubles when she was a new ship.

Her last "seagoing" was in the summer of 1881, when Commander E. U. Shepard took her to sea. Then the training program was changed, and there seemed no place in it for a sailing vessel.

*Constitution* was docked at the New York Navy yard and kept there for two years, during which time her canvas rotted and her rigging grew loose. So when it came time to move her to Portsmouth, New Hampshire, to become a receiving ship, the Navy estimated costs (and considered the problem of finding enough deepwater sailing men to sail her) and then had her towed up to Portsmouth by a steamer. As a receiving ship, she took in young recruits to the service and gave them a taste of naval life right from the beginning. It was still a useful service, if no longer a glamorous one.

There was a touch of the old times in the fall of 1897. The navy had not forgotten. On September 21 she arrived (under tow again) at Boston Navy Yard, for the celebration of the one hundredth anniversary of her launching. The big steam warships *New York*, *Brooklyn*, *Iowa*, *Massachusetts*, and *Texas* all came up and anchored in Boston port for the celebration.

The Mayor of Boston came out for the party, and so did an assistant secretary of the navy, and a meeting was staged at the Old South Meeting House, where a dozen politicians and civic leaders made speeches honoring the grand old vessel and her glorious history.

Then came events that caused *Constitution* to lie forgotten in Boston port. The Spanish-American war broke out in 1898, and *Constitution*'s old captain George Dewey destroyed the Spanish fleet in Manila Bay, while other American fighting men knocked the remainder of the enemy's naval might off Santiago de Cuba.

It was a day of steel ships and steam, and when the battleship *Oregon* raced around the tip of South America in record time to join the Cuban action, *Oregon* became the symbol of American naval might. *Constitution* was pushed into the background.

She might have been forgotten completely and broken up, had it not been for the Massachusetts Daughters of the War of 1812. For in 1900, seeing her moldering in the harbor, and hearing ominous talk of "the old wreck" these ladies of Boston and other cities of Massachusetts started a drive for money to repair and restore the grand ship to the way she was in her days of glory. In 1900 Congress approved the proposition, provided the ladies could raise at least $400,000, which was an immense sum.

It was so large a sum in fact that the workers failed to raise it, but they created so much interest that Congress was persuaded a few years later to appropriate $100,000. Altogether there was enough money to remove the strange housing that had been put on her deck in those years when she was made into a store ship and a training ship, to take out the steam heat, to put in some replicas of her old guns, and to replace the rigging, spars and some of the woodwork as it had been. It was not a complete restoration by any means, but it was enough to give people a feeling for the old frigates, and the days of sail. She was turned into a floating museum.

In 1917 when World War I stirred the nation, someone in the navy had the idea of changing her name to *Old Constitution*, so a new battle cruiser could be given the fine old name. Fortunately, the war ended before this happened — and her name was given back to her. After that, no one seriously considered taking the name away again.

Ten years later, she was really restored, through a combination of gifts made by Americans. A movement was begun among the school children of America to raise money. Gordon Grant, a famous artist of the day, painted a picture of the *Constitution* showing her under sail, and this was reproduced and millions of copies made to sell and raise money. Motion picture producer Jesse Lasky made a film about *Old Ironsides* and this raised more money. Five million school children saved pennies for the fund. And on July 16, 1927, the old ship was towed into the Boston dry dock with a twenty-one-gun salute and a fine patriotic ceremony, witnessed by thousands who had come to cheer her on. Three years later the work was finished as far as it could go there with the money on hand, and she sailed out, flying her flags proudly at mainmast and bowsprit. Congress appropriated another $300,000 and she was completely refurbished as a United States frigate, and was commissioned once more as an active ship in the United States Navy, captained by a naval officer, and manned by a naval crew.

The American Legion was holding its national convention in Boston when the commissioning ceremony came, and she was towed around Boston harbor, with her pennants and flags flying, and the naval vessels in the harbor saluted her while the shore rang with the cheers of the people who had come for the ceremony.

For the next three years, *Constitution* sailed from one American port to another, from the Atlantic to the Pacific and into the Caribbean and the Gulf of Mexico. She had officers and a crew of forty-two sailing men, and lecturers told her great story to the school children and visitors who flocked to see her at every port. Millions of people went aboard — at San Pedro alone she entertained nearly 500,000 visitors in less than a month, and she had similar welcomes in ports of twenty-one states.

Then *Constitution* came back to Boston in 1934, once more to be a museum and a part of the historic life of that famous American city.

In 1940 *Constitution* was again commissioned and a week after Pearl Harbor a memorial service was held aboard her to commemorate the one hundred men killed in the sinking of the destroyer *Reuben James* — the navy could give no more fitting tribute to its heroes than to honor them there, aboard *Constitution*.

For a time during the war, *Constitution* was the flagship of Admiral Ernest J. King, the commander in chief of the navy. At the end of the war she became flagship of the commandant of the First Naval District.

Today she is in Boston, the oldest ship on the Navy List, and one of the stops on the famous Freedom Trail of Boston, a reminder of the greatest days of America's sailing navy.

# Notes and Bibliography

The author is indebted to Vice Admiral Edwin Hooper USN, Ret., Director of Naval History, and several officers of the Naval History division in Washington for information and material used in this book on *Constitution*.

Many books give aspects of the story of *Old Ironsides* and her fighting men. The following reading list may be helpful:

*The Frigate Constitution*, by Ira N. Hollis, Houghton Mifflin Co., Boston, 1900.

*Life in a Man of* War, by Henry J. Mercier. Houghton Mifflin Co., Boston.

*The History of Our Navy* (4 vols), by John R. Spears. Charles Scribner's Sons, New York, 1897.

*Old Ironsides*, by Harry Hansen. Random House, New York, 1955.

*Twenty-Six Historic Ships*, by Frederick Stanhope Hill. G. P. Putnam's Sons, New York, 1903.

*Old Ironsides*, by John De Morgan. McLoughlin Bros., Springfield, Mass., 1933.

*The History of the American Sailing Navy*, by Howard L. Chappelle. Bonanza Books, New York, 1949.

The employees of G.K. Hall hope you have enjoyed this Large Print book. All our Large Print titles are designed for easy reading, and all our books are made to last. Other G.K. Hall books are available at your library, through selected bookstores, or directly from us.

For information about titles, please call:

(800) 223-1244
(800) 223-6121

To share your comments, please write:

Publisher
G.K. Hall & Co.
P.O. Box 159
Thorndike, ME  04986